Bible Nurture and Reader Series

From a child thou hast known
The HOLY SCRIPTURES
which are able to make
thee wise unto salvation.

Bible Nurture and Reader Series

God Leads His People

Grade 3

Units 1, 2, 3

Rod and Staff Publishers, Inc.
Crockett, Kentucky 41413

Telephone (606) 522-4348

BIBLE NURTURE AND READER SERIES

"If you train your children carefully until they are seven years old, they are already three-quarters educated." This quote recognizes the importance of the critical early years in molding a child's life. The influences of childhood become powerful, lasting impressions.

The type of schoolbooks used certainly affects the developing appetites of our children for reading material. We will not instill in them appreciation for godly values by feeding them frivolous nonsense. We hold the Bible to be the highest guide for life and the best source of training for our children. The Bible reveals God and His will. Proverbs 9:10 says, "The fear of the Lord is the beginning of wisdom: and the knowledge of the holy is understanding." It is important that our children are exposed to truth from the beginning of their learning experience.

For the student to be exposed to the truth of God's Word only in textbooks is not sufficient to give him the very best. It is necessary for the tutor, be he parent or other teacher, to be firmly rooted in the Word of God and have the power of God's presence in his life. The Bible must be treasured as God's message to mankind. On that conviction this series is built, with the Scriptures as its very substance.

This book is designed as part of a series and will be most effective if so used. The grade three material includes the following books.

Teacher's Manual	Reading Workbook Unit 1
	Reading Workbook Unit 2
Pupil's Reader Units 1–3	Reading Workbook Unit 3
Pupil's Reader Units 4, 5	Reading Workbook Unit 4
	Reading Workbook Unit 5

Copyright, 1988

First edition, copyright 1964; revisions 1971, 1987

By
Rod and Staff Publishers, Inc.
Crockett, Kentucky 41413

Printed in U. S. A.

ISBN 0-7399-0384-5

Catalog no. 11301.3

12   13   14   15   16   —   16   15   14   13   12   11   10   09   08   07

Table of Contents

Unit 1

Stories About David and Solomon

Unit 2

Stories of the Kings— Rehoboam to Jehoram

Unit 3

Stories of the Last Kings and the Prophets

Unit One

Stories About David and Solomon

David Mourns for Saul

2 Samuel 1:1–16

King Saul, the first king of Israel, was dead. He had started out to be a good king, but he did not continue in the right way. He had not been careful to obey God in everything. Instead, he had foolishly taken his own way. He was wounded in battle, and then he killed himself. His life ended very sadly.

Before King Saul died, God had chosen David to be king after Saul's death. Saul had seen that the Lord was with David and was blessing him. He had seen, too, that the people of Israel loved and honored David more than himself. Saul had been very jealous of David and had often tried to kill him. But God had always taken care of David. King Saul had never been able to kill him. David would be king according to God's plan.

David was not in the land of Israel during the battle in which Saul died. He had not heard that Saul and three of his sons were dead. David's good friend Jonathan was one of Saul's three sons that had been killed in battle.

After the battle, a young man came to David. To show sorrow, he came with his clothes torn and with dirt on his head. He fell down on the ground before David and gave him honor.

David asked him, "From where did you come?"

"I escaped out of the camp of Israel," the young man replied.

"How did the battle go?" asked David. "Please tell me."

"The people ran away from the battle," said the young man. "Many have fallen and are dead. Saul and his son Jonathan are dead also."

"How do you know that Saul and Jonathan are dead?" David asked.

The young man answered, "As I happened to come on Mount Gilboa, Saul leaned on his spear. The chariots and the horsemen were following him. Saul looked behind him and saw me. He called to me. I answered, 'Here I am.' He asked, 'Who are you?' I answered, 'I am an Amalekite.' Saul said to me, 'Please kill me, for I am badly hurt and yet I am alive and suffering.' So I killed him because I was sure that he would die anyway. I took the crown that was on his head and the bracelet that was on his arm. I have brought them to you."

Not all of this story that the young man told David was true. It was indeed true that Saul and Jonathan were dead. But it was not true that this young man had killed Saul. Saul had asked his helper to kill him. But his helper had been afraid to do it. So Saul had killed himself. This young man made up the story because he thought that David would be glad to hear that Saul was dead. He thought that David would give him a reward for bringing him this news.

But he was greatly mistaken. He did not know God's thoughts as David did. David knew that God had anointed Saul to be king. He knew that God wanted him to honor Saul as God's anointed one, no matter how mean he was. He knew it was a very serious thing to kill God's anointed king.

David and his men tore their clothes in sorrow. They wept and would not eat. They were in great sorrow because King Saul and his son Jonathan and many of God's people had been killed.

David asked the young man, "Why were you not afraid to kill the Lord's anointed?" The young man had no good answer to give David. David had the young man killed because of what he said he had done.

David Anointed King Over Judah

2 Samuel 2

David was in the land of the Philistines when he heard that Saul and Jonathan were dead. The Philistines lived close to the land of Israel, but they were always enemies to them. It was the Philistines who had killed Saul's sons and many of the people of Israel.

David had fled into the Philistines' land so that Saul could not find him to kill him. For a year and four months he had been in the land of the Philistines. Now he wanted to go back to his own land. But he did not go without asking the Lord if he should go. He asked, "Shall I go up into any of the cities of Judah?"

The Lord said to David, "Go."

David knew now that he should go to his homeland. But he still did not know to which city of Judah he should go. He could have decided that for himself, but that would not have been safe. David wanted to be only where the Lord wanted him to be. He asked the Lord, "Where shall I go?"

"To Hebron," the Lord answered. Hebron was an old city. It was about fourteen miles south of Bethlehem, David's home town.

David, his wives, and the men who were with him went to Hebron to live. There the men of Judah, David's own tribe, came and anointed him to be king. David was thirty years old when he was anointed king over Judah.

David was king over only the tribe of Judah. He did not rule over the rest of the tribes of Israel. The tribe of Judah lived in the country around Jerusalem, Bethlehem, and Hebron. God had given them this part of the land of Canaan. The other tribes lived farther north and across the Jordan River.

The men of Judah said to David, "The men of Jabesh-gilead have buried Saul." Jabesh-gilead was a city across the Jordan River. It was in the country that belonged to the tribe of Gad. The men of Jabesh-gilead had heard what the Philistines had done to King Saul. Their brave men had gone at night and had taken Saul's body and the bodies of his sons from the Philistines. They buried their bodies under a tree at Jabesh.

David was pleased that the men of Jabesh-gilead had shown this kindness to Saul. He sent

messengers to them with kind words to bless them.

The tribe of Judah had David for their king. Abner, Saul's captain, made Ish-bosheth, one of Saul's sons, king over the other tribes of Israel. Ish-bosheth was forty years old when he was made king. He reigned as king for two years.

The people who followed King David and the people who followed King Ish-bosheth did not get along together peaceably. There were many wars between them.

One day Abner, Ish-bosheth's captain, and his men gathered together at Gibeon, where there was a large pool of water. Joab, David's captain, and his men met them there on the opposite side of the pool. They sat down. Abner wanted to see twelve of his men fight with twelve of Joab's men. Abner said, "Let the young men arise and play before us."

Joab said, "Let them arise."

Twelve men from each side fought together and killed one another. But the fighting did not stop there. There was a terrible battle between the two sides. Abner's men were beaten by Joab's men, but Abner himself was not killed. Abner and his men ran away.

Asahel, Joab's brother, ran after Abner. He was as light of foot as a wild deer and could run very fast.

Abner looked behind him to see who was chasing him. He said, "Are you Asahel?"

Asahel answered, "I am."

Abner did not want to kill Asahel. But he did not want Asahel to kill him either. So, because Asahel followed to kill him, he killed Asahel with the back end of his spear.

Joab and another of his brothers went after Abner. When the sun went down, they came to where Abner and his group of men were. They were on the top of a hill. Abner called to Joab and persuaded Joab to quit following them. He warned them that if they kept on, it would mean bitterness in the end.

Joab then blew the trumpet, and all his people stood still. They did not try to fight with Abner and his men any more.

Altogether, twenty of David's men had been killed, but three hundred sixty of Abner's men were killed.

Abner Is Slain

2 Samuel 3

For a long time there was war between those who followed David and those who followed Saul's son Ish-bosheth. David's group became stronger and stronger. Ish-bosheth's group became weaker and weaker, even though eleven tribes followed him and only one tribe followed David. This was because it was God's will that David should have the kingdom. He had taken it from Saul and had given it to David.

Abner kept trying to help Ish-bosheth have a strong kingdom. But one day something happened to change this. King Ish-bosheth accused Abner of doing a very wicked deed. Abner became very angry. He had worked hard to help Ish-bosheth. Now Ish-bosheth was accusing him of sin. Abner warned King Ish-bosheth, "Your kingdom will be taken away from you and given to David." Then King Ish-bosheth was afraid to say anything more to Abner.

After this Abner sent messengers to King

David to make an agreement with him. They brought King David this message from Abner, "Make an agreement with me, and I will help you to be king over all Israel."

David answered, "I will make an agreement with you. But one thing you must do. You must bring Michal, Saul's daughter, when you come to see me. Unless you do, you shall not see my face."

David also sent messengers to King Ish-bosheth, saying, "Give me back my wife Michal." Saul had given Michal to David to be his wife. Then later he took her away from David and gave her to another man to be his wife.

Ish-bosheth did as David said. He took Michal away from the husband with whom she was living to give her back to David.

The man was very sad to have Michal taken away from him. He followed after Michal, weeping as he went. Finally Abner told him to go back home, and he went.

Abner talked to some of the older men of Israel. He said, "You tried before to have David to be king over you. Now do it, for this is what God has said, 'I will use David to save My people Israel from all their enemies.'"

Then Abner went to speak to King David.

David made a feast for Abner and his men. Abner said to David, "I will gather the people of Israel to you so that you can be king over them." Then King David sent Abner away in peace.

Joab and his men were gone when Abner talked to King David. When they came back, they heard that Abner had been there. They heard, too, that David had sent Abner away in peace.

This displeased Joab. He came to King David and said, "What have you done? Abner came to you. Why have you sent him away? You know Abner. He came to deceive you and to find out all that you are doing."

Then without telling David, Joab sent men after Abner to bring him back to Hebron. When Abner came back, Joab pretended that he wanted to tell him a secret. He took Abner aside in the gate. There Joab smote Abner and killed him because he had killed his brother Asahel.

When David heard what Joab had done, he was greatly displeased. He did not want any part in the guilt of slaying Abner. The guilt was on Joab and on his father's family.

David said to Joab and to everyone who was with him, "Tear your clothes and put on sackcloth. Mourn for Abner." David followed the casket as they went to bury Abner. He and all the people wept at the grave. The people understood very well that David was not the one who wanted Abner killed.

David said to the people, "Do you know that a prince and a great man has fallen in Israel today? God will punish the one who has done this wicked deed."

David Becomes King
Over All Israel

2 Samuel 4:1–5:16; 1 Chronicles 11:1–9

King Ish-bosheth heard that Abner, his captain, was dead in Hebron. This made him feel very weak and helpless. All the people of Israel were troubled. No one knew what to do. Two of the captains of King Ish-bosheth fled with their families into another country to live.

One day these two captains came back to the house of King Ish-bosheth. They came at noon when the king was lying on his bed. They acted as though they were doing some business for the king. But they did not do the king's business. Instead, they went into the bedroom of King Ish-bosheth and killed him. Then they cut off his head, took it with them, and escaped out of the house.

The two captains took the head of King Ish-bosheth to King David. They said to David, "See the head of Ish-bosheth, the son of Saul your enemy, who tried to kill you."

The captains thought that David would be pleased that they had killed a son of Saul. But David was not pleased. Righteous men are not pleased with any unkindness to anyone. David said, "When someone told me that Saul was dead, thinking he was bringing good news, I killed him. How much more shall I kill wicked men who have slain a righteous man in his own house upon his bed?"

David commanded his young men to kill these two captains for their wicked deed. Then David buried the head of King Ish-bosheth in Abner's gave at Hebron.

Now all the tribes of Israel were ready to let David be their king. They came to David in Hebron. They said, "In times past when Saul was king over us, you were the one that led Israel. And the Lord said to you, 'You shall feed My people Israel, and you shall be captain over them.' " They knew that it was God's will that David should be their king.

David knew, too, that God had called him to be king over all the tribes. He had already been king over the tribe of Judah for seven and one-half years. Now he was anointed king over all the twelve tribes. While he had been king over the tribe of Judah only, he lived at Hebron. Now after he became king over all Israel, he wanted to move to Jerusalem.

But enemies of Israel lived at Jerusalem. They did not want to let David come into their city. They thought that they could keep David out.

David said to his people, "Whoever will kill the people in Jerusalem will be chief and captain."

Joab went up first and killed them, so he was made chief and captain. David then went to Jerusalem to live and to reign. For thirty-three years he reigned over all Israel. All the tribes were now one kingdom. Their king lived at Jerusalem. It was then called the city of David. The Lord was with David, and he became a great man.

Hiram, king of another country, sent messengers to David. He also sent cedar trees, carpenters, and masons. The carpenters and masons built a house of cedar for David at Jerusalem.

Now David knew that God had made his kingdom great and strong and sure. It was God who had made him king over Israel. He had not killed any of Saul's family so that he could be king. He had waited on God. He had waited until the people were ready to let him rule over them.

David knew that God had made the kingdom great for the sake of His people Israel.

While David lived at Jerusalem, eleven more sons were born to him. These, with the six sons born at Hebron, made him seventeen sons.

David Brings the
Ark to Jerusalem

2 Samuel 5:17–6:18

When the Philistines heard that David was made king over all Israel and Judah, they came to fight against him. David heard of it and went to a place of protection called a hold.

Now the Philistines had gathered together for battle in a field full of barley. All the people of Israel had fled from before them and had hid themselves.

David asked the Lord, "Shall I go up to the Philistines? Will You deliver them into my hand?"

"You may go," the Lord answered. "I will surely deliver the Philistines into your hand."

So David and his mighty men set themselves in the middle of the barley field. They killed the Philistines. The Lord gave His people a great deliverance.

The Philistines had taken idols with them to battle. As they fled from David, they left their images behind. David and his men burned them.

After this, the Philistines came again and spread themselves in the valley. David asked the Lord again what he should do.

The Lord said, "Go behind the Philistines over by the mulberry trees. When you hear the sound of a going in the mulberry trees, stir yourselves. The Lord will then go before you to kill the Philistines."

David did as the Lord commanded him. Again the Lord gave Israel a great deliverance from their enemies.

For a long time Israel had many wars with the Philistines. At last the wars were over for a while. There was peace in the land of Israel. David could now think about other things.

David thought about the ark of God. It was still where the people of Israel had put it after the Philistines sent it back to Israel. That was in the days when Samuel was still living. David talked to all the people of Israel. He said, "If it seems good to you and if the Lord our God wants us to do this, let us bring again the ark of our God to us." Everyone thought it was time to bring the ark to Jerusalem.

So David gathered together all the chosen

men of Israel. This was thirty thousand men. They went with David to bring the ark of God to Jerusalem.

The men set the ark of God upon a new cart which was pulled by oxen. They started back to Jerusalem. On the way the oxen stumbled. This shook the ark. Uzzah, one of the men who was driving the cart, put out his hand to steady the ark. This was a very serious thing to do. No one was supposed to touch the ark. God had told the priests to carry the ark with staves. It was not to be carried on a cart. So God was not pleased when Uzzah put his hand on the ark of God to hold it steady. God caused Uzzah to die for doing this.

David was afraid because of what God did to Uzzah. He said, "How shall I bring the ark of God home to me?"

So they did not bring the ark all the way home to Jerusalem. Instead David left it at the home of Obed-edom, a man who lived nearby. For three months the ark stayed with the family of Obed-edom. God blessed the house of Obed-edom because His ark was there.

Someone came to David. He said, "The Lord has blessed the house of Obed-edom because of the ark of God."

David was now ready to bring the ark all the way back to Jerusalem. He had a tent set up to put it in. This time he was careful to have the ark carried as God said that it should be carried. He sent priests and Levites to bring the ark. The priests carried the ark on their shoulders with staves. This was the way that God had told Moses it should be carried. Now the ark was brought with great joy, for to obey God always brings joy.

Before they had gone far, David stopped to sacrifice oxen and other animals to the Lord. At last the ark was in Jerusalem in the tent that David had prepared for it. Again David offered burnt offerings and peace offerings to the Lord. He then blessed the people in the Name of the Lord.

God Makes Great
Promises to David

2 Samuel 7

One day David was sitting in his house. He was talking to Nathan the prophet. He said, "See, I live in a house of cedar, but God's house is in a tent." It did not seem right to David that he should live in a nice cedar house while the ark of God was in a tent. He wanted to build a house for God.

Nathan told King David, "Go and do what you would like to do. The Lord is with you."

But God did not want David to build Him a house. David had been a man of war, and God wanted a man of peace to build a house for Him. Yet God was pleased that David loved Him and wanted to build a house for Him.

That night God talked to Nathan the prophet. He told him to go to King David with this message: "This is what the Lord says, 'Shall you build Me a house? I have not lived in a house since

I brought Israel up out of Egypt. I have never told My people to build Me a house of cedar, but I have walked in a tent. Did I ever say to My people, "Why do you not build Me a house of cedar?" You shall not make Me a house. I will make you a house.' "

God went on with the message that He wanted Nathan to give to David. He said, "Tell David, 'When you are dead, your son will be king. He will build Me a house. I will make his kingdom stand forever.' " Yes, God would never take the kingdom away from David or from his sons. He had taken the kingdom away from Saul, but He would make David's kingdom stand forever.

Do you know how God made David a house and a kingdom that will stand forever? God gave David a family. Jesus came from David's line of children, or family. Jesus is a king who will reign for ever and ever.

Nathan the prophet went to King David. He told David what the Lord said.

David was surprised with this message from God. But he wanted the Lord to do exactly what He thought best, even if he could not build a house for God. He was thankful for God's great promises to him. He was especially thankful that

God would build him a house and make his kingdom stand forever. He was so thankful that he hardly knew what to say.

David said, "Who am I, O Lord God, and what is my house that You have promised me these things? It is because of what You have spoken and want. You are great, O Lord God. There is none like You; neither is there any God beside You. And what nation in the earth is like Your people, even like Israel? You redeemed them from Egypt to be Your people forever. You have become their God. Now, O Lord God, let Your Name be magnified and let the house of Your servant David stand forever. For, O Lord God of Israel, You have shown this to me. You have said, 'I will build you a house.' For this reason I have prayed this prayer to You. And now, O Lord God, You are that God; and Your words are true. You have promised this goodness to me. Let it please You to bless my house that it may continue forever, for You have said that it would. With Your blessing let me be blessed forever."

David Shows Kindness to Others

2 Samuel 9:1–10:5

King David remembered the people who had been kind to him. He was thankful for each kindness, and he wanted to show kindness to them in return.

David thought about his good friend Jonathan. He wanted to be kind to Jonathan's family because Jonathan had been kind to him. David asked, "Is there any of Saul's house who are still alive?"

"Yes," someone told him, "Saul has a servant who is yet living. His name is Ziba." So David called for Ziba.

When Ziba came in, the king asked, "Are you Ziba?"

Ziba answered, "Your servant is he."

David said, "Is there any left yet of Saul's family that I can show the kindness of God to him?"

Ziba answered, "Jonathan has a son who is lame on his feet. His name is Mephibosheth."

36

When Mephibosheth was five years old, the message had come that Jonathan and Saul had been killed. His nurse had picked him up and hurried to run away. In her haste she had dropped little Mephibosheth. From that time on, he was lame on both feet.

David asked Ziba, "Where is he?"

Ziba told David where Mephibosheth was, and David sent for him.

Mephibosheth came to King David. He bowed before him and showed much respect.

David said, "Mephibosheth."

"Behold your servant," answered Mephibosheth.

David said, "Do not be afraid. I will surely be kind to you for the sake of your father Jonathan. I will give you back all the land that belonged to your grandfather Saul. You can eat at my table all the time."

Mephibosheth bowed again before King David. He did not understand why David should be so kind to him. He said, "Who am I that you should look upon such a dead dog as I am?" Being lame on both feet, he felt he was worth nothing to David. He could not work for him as other servants could.

King David called Ziba to him again. He said, "I have given Mephibosheth everything that was Saul's. You and your sons and your servants shall farm the land for him. You shall harvest the crops. Mephibosheth will always eat at my table like one of the king's sons."

Ziba said to the king, "As you have commanded me, so shall I do." Ziba had fifteen sons and twenty servants to help him in this work.

So Jonathan's son, Mephibosheth, lived in Jerusalem. Every day he ate at the king's table as one of King David's sons. Yet he was lame on both feet.

After this, David heard that the king of the children of Ammon had died. His son, Hanun, had become king in his place. Since Hanun's father had been kind to David, David wanted to show kindness to his son. So David sent some of his servants to Hanun to comfort him because his father had died. The servants came into the land where Hanun was king.

But the princes of the children of Ammon did not trust David's servants. They said to King Hanun, "Do you think that David is honoring your father by sending comforters to you? Has not David rather sent men to search and spy out the city and destroy it?"

Hanun believed his princes. He thought that David's servants only pretended that they had come to comfort him. He was mean to them and treated them shamefully. He shaved off one-half of each man's beard and cut off part of their clothes. David's servants felt greatly ashamed. They looked strange with half a beard on their faces and with only part of their clothes. They had come to show kindness to Hanun, but Hanun treated them very unkindly.

When King David heard how shamefully they had been treated, he felt sorry for them. He could see how ashamed they would be to come home. He told them they could stay at Jericho until their beards grew out again.

1

David Displeases God

2 Samuel 10:6–11:27

The children of Ammon knew that King David was much displeased with them because of the way they had treated David's servants. They decided to fight against Israel. They hired their neighbors, the Syrians, to help them in the battle. Altogether, they hired thirty-three thousand men.

David heard that the children of Ammon had come to fight against him. He sent out his men to fight with them. Joab went as their captain.

Joab saw that both the Syrians and the children of Ammon had come to fight against them. One army was in front of him. The other army was behind him. Joab chose his best men to fight against the Syrians. Joab was their captain. He let the rest of the men fight against the children of Ammon. Joab's brother was their captain.

Joab said to his brother, "If the Syrians are too strong for me, then you shall help me. But if the children of Ammon are too strong for you, then I will come and help you. Be of good courage. Let us be strong like men for the sake of our people and for the sake of the cities of our God. The Lord will do whatever seems good to Him."

When Joab and his men came near to the Syrians, the Syrians were afraid and ran away. When the children of Ammon saw that the Syrians fled, they, too, became afraid and fled. Many Syrians were killed, but most of the children of Ammon escaped. When the king of Syria and the king of Ammon saw that they were beaten, they made peace with Israel and became Israel's servants.

Some time after the battle in which many Syrians had been killed, David sent Joab and all Israel to destroy the children of Ammon. The kings themselves used to go along out to battle, but David did not go with them to this battle. He stayed in Jerusalem.

One evening David got up from his bed. He walked on the roof of his house. From the roof he saw a beautiful woman. He wanted to know who she was. When David asked about her, someone told him, "Her name is Bath-sheba. She is the wife of Uriah."

David knew it is wrong for a man to have

another man's wife. That is adultery. The seventh one of the Ten Commandments says, "Thou shalt not commit adultery." But David wanted this beautiful woman. She belonged to Uriah, so David broke another commandment by coveting her. The last of the Ten Commandments says, "Thou shalt not covet."

One sin brings more sins. Now David planned how to get Bath-sheba. He decided to have Uriah killed. Then he could have Bath-sheba for his wife. This was breaking the sixth commandment, which says, "Thou shalt not kill."

One morning David wrote a letter to Joab, the captain of his army. This is what the letter said: "Put Uriah in the front of the hottest battle. Leave him there by himself so that he will be killed."

David sent this letter with Uriah for him to give to his captain, Joab. Uriah did not know what was in the letter. He faithfully took the letter to his captain.

Joab read the letter. He did not know why King David asked this of him, but he did as David commanded him. He looked over the city. Then he placed Uriah where the brave men were. The men of the city came to fight with Israel. Uriah and some other soldiers were killed.

After this Joab called a messenger to him. He said, "Tell David what happened in the battle. If the king is angry and asks, 'Why did you go so near to the city to fight? Did you not know that they would shoot from the wall?' then you shall say, 'Your servant Uriah is dead also.'"

The messenger went to King David. He told David about the battle. He told him that Uriah was dead.

David did not become angry. He said to the messenger, "Tell Joab, 'Do not be displeased. The sword kills one as well as another.' Encourage Joab to make the battle stronger and to destroy the city."

Now King David knew that Uriah was dead. Bath-sheba also heard that her husband was dead, and she mourned for him. When she had finished mourning, David sent for her to come to his house. She came to his house and became his wife. A little son was born to them.

But the thing that David had done displeased the Lord very much.

Lesson 9

"You Are the Man"

2 Samuel 12:1–14

The Lord sent the prophet Nathan to David. Nathan came to David and told him this story:

"There were two men in one city. The one man was rich, and the other man was poor. The rich man had exceeding many flocks and herds. But the poor man had nothing except one little ewe lamb. He had raised this little lamb and fed it. It grew up together with him and his children. It ate of his own food. It drank of his cup. It lay in his lap and was like a daughter to him.

"A traveler came to the rich man. The rich man wanted to kill a lamb and make a good meal for the traveler. But he did not take an animal of his own flock or of his own herd to prepare for the traveler. Instead, he took the poor man's only ewe lamb."

As David listened to this story, he became very angry with the rich man. "How cruel," he thought, "for the rich man to take this poor man's only pet lamb when he had so many lambs of his own!" David said to Nathan, "As the Lord lives, the man who did this thing shall surely die. And he shall give back four lambs for the one he took, because he did this and had no pity."

Nathan said to David, "You are the man."

What a shock this must have been for David! How could he be that cruel rich man?

Nathan went on to tell David how this was. First he showed David how rich he was. He said, "This is what the Lord says, 'I anointed you to be king over Israel. I delivered you out of the hand of Saul. I gave you your master's house and his wives. I gave you the house of Israel and of Judah. And if this had not been enough, I would have given you more things.' "

Nathan went on with the Lord's message to David. He said, " 'Why have you despised the commandment of the Lord to do this evil in His sight? You have killed Uriah with the sword and have taken his wife to be your wife. Because you have despised Me and have taken his wife to be your wife, the sword will never depart from your house. You did your wicked deed secretly, but I will punish you before all Israel.' "

Now David saw what a very wicked thing he had done. Truly he was a rich man. God had been very good to him. But he had sinned against God and had been very cruel to Uriah. He had taken away his wife. He had caused him to be killed. David was very sorry for what he had done. He said to Nathan, "I have sinned against the Lord."

Nathan said to David, "The Lord has put away your sin. You will not die. But because you have done this thing, you have given great cause for God's enemies to speak evil. Also, the child that is born to you shall surely die."

Yes, because David was sorry for his sin, God forgave him. But David would suffer greatly for his sin. His family would also have to suffer.

After Nathan's visit to David, David wrote Psalm 51. Maybe you would like to read it.

David Suffers for His Sin

2 Samuel 12:15–24

Nathan had told David that his child would die. So the Lord caused the child to become very sick.

David was very sad when his child became sick. He would not eat. He lay down all night upon the ground. He prayed to God for his child. He thought perhaps God would have pity on him and would let the child live after all.

The older men in David's house went to David to raise him up from the ground. But David would not listen to them. He would not get up from the ground. Neither would he eat with them.

For seven days the child was sick. On the seventh day, he died. While the child was still alive, David had been so sad and had acted strangely. What might he do to himself when he heard that the child was dead? David's servants did not know. They were afraid to tell David that his child was dead.

The servants whispered to one another about

the child. They did not want David to hear what they said. But David saw that they were whispering, and he thought that his child must be dead. He asked them, "Is the child dead?"

They answered, "He is dead."

When David heard this, he got up from the earth. He washed his face and changed his clothes. He went to the house of God and worshiped the Lord. When he came home again, he asked his servants to set food before him. They set food before him, and he ate.

The servants were puzzled. Why did David feel better after he heard that his child was dead? They could not understand this. They came to David and said, "What is this that you have done? You fasted and wept for the child when he was alive. But when the child is dead, you get up and eat."

David answered, "While the child was yet alive, I fasted and wept; for I said, 'Who can tell if God will be kind to me that the child may live?' But now he is dead, so why should I fast? Can I bring him back again? I shall go to him, but he shall not return to me."

David knew that it would do no good to pray to God to heal the child after the child was dead.

God had done to the child what He had said He would do. David knew that he would never see his child again on this earth. Now he looked forward to the time when he would go to be with his child.

David comforted Bath-sheba his wife after their son died. The Lord was good to them and gave them other sons. David named the first of them Solomon. His name means "peaceable and perfect."

The Bible tells us that the Lord loved Solomon.

Wicked Absalom

2 Samuel 13:1–14:29

David had many sons. Some of them were wicked men. One of David's wicked sons was Absalom. Absalom hated his half brother Amnon because Amnon had done a wicked deed. Absalom wanted to kill Amnon.

Two years passed after Amnon had done his wicked deed. At this time Absalom had men to cut the wool off his sheep. These men were called sheepshearers. Absalom invited all the king's sons to go with him to where the sheepshearers were. He came also to his father David and said, "I have men to cut the wool off my sheep. Please come, you and your servants, with me."

But King David, his father, said, "No, my son, let us not all go now."

Absalom still begged his father to go along. Still David would not go, but he did bless his son.

Then Absalom said, "If you will not go, please let my brother Amnon go with us."

"Why should he go?" asked King David.

But Absalom begged his father until David let Amnon and the rest of his sons go with Absalom.

Now Absalom had commanded his servants, "When I tell you to kill Amnon, kill him. Do not be afraid. Have I not told you to do this?"

When all the king's sons were together, Absalom gave his servants word to kill Amnon. The servants did as they were told. All the rest of the king's sons got on their mules and fled. They did not want to be killed, too.

While they were fleeing on their mules, someone came to David. He said, "Absalom has killed all the king's sons. Not one of them is left."

When the king heard this, he arose, tore his clothes, and then lay down on the ground. His grief was very great. All his servants stood by with their clothes torn also.

David's nephew came to David. He said, "Do not think that they have killed all the king's sons. Only Amnon is dead."

A young man who was the watchman looked up. He saw many people coming by the way of the hillside that was behind him.

David's nephew said to David, "See, the king's sons are coming. It is just as I told you."

As soon as he had finished talking to David, the king's sons came. They were weeping. The king and his servants were also weeping.

But Absalom fled to another country. He was gone for three years. He was afraid to come home because he had killed his half brother, one of David's sons.

As time went on, David forgot some of his sorrow. He longed to see his son Absalom again. After three years, he sent Joab to get Absalom and bring him back to Jerusalem.

David said, "Let him go to his own house. Do not let him see my face."

So Absalom came back to his house at Jerusalem. But he was not allowed to see his father.

For two years Absalom lived in Jerusalem without seeing his father. Now he wanted to see him. He called for Joab to come to him. He wanted Joab to talk to his father for him.

But Joab would not come. Absalom sent for him the second time. Still Joab would not come.

Then Absalom had his servants do a mean thing to get Joab to come to him.

Absalom Deceives His Father and the People

2 Samuel 14:30–15:12

Two times Absalom had called for Joab to come to him. Yet Joab had not come. So Absalom said to his servants, "See, Joab's field is near mine. He has barley there. Go and set his field on fire."

This soon brought Joab over to Absalom's house. Joab asked Absalom, "Why did your servants set my field on fire?"

Absalom answered, "I sent for you to come, and you would not come. I wanted you to go to the king for me. I wanted you to ask him why he brought me back to Jerusalem if he will not let me see him."

Joab went to King David. He told him what Absalom had said.

King David then called for Absalom to come. When Absalom came, he bowed himself before his father. The king kissed him.

Now Absalom was the most beautiful man of all the children of Israel. He was strong and healthy. He had much hair on his head. At the end of every year he had his hair cut because it was very heavy on his head. The hair that was cut off each year weighed about four to seven pounds.

Although Absalom was handsome on the outside, he was ugly inside. He thought wicked thoughts. He wanted to be a great man. He prepared chariots and horses and fifty men to run before him. He would get up early in the morning and stand beside the way of the gate. People came through this gate to go to King David for help with their problems. As someone came along, Absalom would call to him. He would say, "From what city are you?"

The man would then tell him where he was from.

Then Absalom would say to him, "What you have to say is right and good. But the king has no one in charge to listen to you. Oh, that I were made judge in the land that every man who has any problem would come to me. I would do for him whatever was right."

Then if anyone came and bowed to Absalom,

Absalom would take him by the hand and kiss him. He would speak nice words to him. People then began to think that Absalom was a kind man. They thought that he wanted to help them. They did not know that he was only working to get the people on his side so that he could be king.

One day Absalom said to David, "Please let me go to Hebron. I want to do what I promised the Lord I would do. While I was gone I made a promise to the Lord. I told Him that if He would bring me back to Jerusalem, I would serve Him."

No doubt David was pleased that Absalom wanted to keep his promise and serve the Lord. He said to Absalom, "Go in peace."

But Absalom had lied to his father. He did not really want to go to Hebron to serve God. He wanted to go to Hebron for a wicked reason. He planned to have the people make him king there. He sent men throughout all the tribes of Israel. He told them to tell the people, "As soon as you hear the sound of the trumpet, then you shall say, 'Absalom is reigning in Hebron.'"

Absalom called for two hundred men from Jerusalem to go with him to Hebron. These men went with Absalom, but they did not know why they were going. They did not know that Absalom was going to have them make him king. But they were ready to follow Absalom and do what he said. All the time, more and more people had looked to Absalom for help with their problems.

While Absalom was at Hebron, he sent for one of his father's wise men to come. His name was Ahithophel. Ahithophel had often given good advice to David. Now Absalom wanted him, so that he could give good advice to him instead of his father.

Lesson 13

David Flees From Absalom

2 Samuel 15:13–31

A messenger came to David. He said, "The people are following Absalom."

When David heard this, he knew that it was dangerous for him to stay at Jerusalem. If Absalom had made himself king and the people were following him, no doubt they would try to kill David. David said to his servants that were with him at Jerusalem, "Arise, and let us flee. If we do not, we shall not be able to escape from Absalom. Hurry, or he will come upon us suddenly and kill us with the sword."

David's servants answered, "We are ready to do whatever you choose to do."

The king, all his family, and his servants left Jerusalem. Only ten women stayed behind to keep the house. The king went ahead, and all the people followed him. When they were a little way from Jerusalem, David and the people stopped and waited. The servants passed on beside him. Six hundred men who had come to David from other lands went on ahead of him.

One of these men was Ittai. He had come to David only the day before, so he was indeed a stranger. David felt sorry for him. He had come to David for help in his troubles, and now already David himself was in trouble. Would Ittai really want to stay with him? David asked Ittai, "Why do you also go with us? Go back to your place and stay with the king, because you are a stranger. Since you came only yesterday, should I today make you go up and down with us? Since I am just going where I may go, go back and take your brethren with you. Mercy and truth be with you."

Ittai answered, "As surely as the Lord lives, and as you, the king, live, I will stay right with you, whether we die or live."

So David let Ittai and all his men and the little children that were with them go along. He told them all to pass over the brook Kidron toward the way of the desert. Then all the people passed over the brook. The king also himself passed over the brook Kidron.

Zadok the priest and all the Levites were also with David. They were carrying the ark of God. David said to Zadok, "Carry the ark of God back to the city. If it pleases the Lord, He will bring me again to Jerusalem where the ark of God is and where God lives. But if I do not please Him, let Him do to me whatever He sees is good. I will stay in the plain in the wilderness until I hear from you."

So Zadok and another priest with their sons returned to Jerusalem. They carried the ark of God back to Jerusalem and stayed there.

David and his men went on up Mount Olivet with their heads covered. They were weeping as they went. It was a very sad time for them. Most of the people seemed to be against them.

Someone came and said to David, "Ahithophel is among the men who went with Absalom." This was more sad news for David. David had always trusted Ahithophel to be a faithful man. Whenever Ahithophel gave him advice, David took it as advice from God. So David was greatly disappointed that Ahithophel went along with Absalom. Now Ahithophel would likely give advice to Absalom against him. David prayed to God about this. He said, "O Lord, I pray You, turn Ahithophel's advice into foolishness."

David Hides

2 Samuel 15:32–16:14

At last David reached the top of Mount Olivet, a mountain just a little east of Jerusalem. There David worshiped the Lord.

While David was on Mount Olivet, Hushai, one of David's friends, came to meet him. His clothes were torn, and he had ground upon his head. In this way he showed that he, too, was sharing in David's sorrow.

David did not think that Hushai could help him by staying with him. He thought that he could be of more help to him by going back home. He wanted him to go to Absalom and pretend to be Absalom's friend. When Ahithophel would give Absalom advice against David, he wanted Hushai to keep Absalom from following Ahithophel's advice.

David told Hushai, "Say to Absalom, 'I will be your servant, O King. As I have been your father's servant up to this time, so will I also now be your servant.' In this way you can keep him from taking Ahithophel's advice. Will not the two priests be with you there? Therefore, whatever you hear in the king's house, you shall tell to the priests. The priests have with them their two sons. Let them bring a message to me of everything that you hear." By doing this, David could hear what Absalom and his men planned to do against him. Then he could escape from them.

Hushai was willing to do this for David. He obediently went back to the city.

Now David started to go down the other side of Mount Olivet. On the way down, Ziba met him. He had with him two donkeys. The donkeys had saddles on them and were loaded with food. There were two hundred loaves of bread, a hundred bunches of raisins, a hundred summer fruits, and a bottle of wine.

The king asked Ziba, "Why did you bring these?"

Ziba answered, "The donkeys are for the king's family to ride on. The bread and the summer fruits are for the young men to eat. The wine is for those who may become faint in the wilderness."

"And where is Mephibosheth?" asked King

David.

Ziba answered, "Mephibosheth is still at Jerusalem. He stayed there because he thinks that Saul's kingdom will be given to him."

These words made David think that even Mephibosheth had turned against him. David said to Ziba, "You can have the things that belonged to Mephibosheth."

Ziba was pleased hear this. But what Ziba said about Mephibosheth was not true. Mephibosheth had not really turned against David.

As David walked on, Shimei, a man of the family of Saul, came and cursed David. He said, "Come out, come out, you bloody man, you man of Belial." *Belial* means "a worthless and a wicked man." As Shimei cursed, he also threw stones and dust at King David and at all his servants.

Joab's brother said to David, "Why should this dead dog curse my lord, the king? Please let me go over and take off his head."

But David did not want to do evil to him. He wanted to leave this man's punishment in the hands of the Lord. David said, "The Lord has told him to curse me. Who then shall ask, 'Why have you done it?'" David did not think it strange that this man cursed him. He said, "My own son is seeking to kill me. How much more may this man do it. It may be that the Lord will look on me and pay me back good for his cursing."

David and his men kept on walking. Shimei kept following along on the hillside nearby, cursing and throwing stones and dust into the air as he went.

At last the king and all the people with him came to a place where they could rest themselves. They were very weary.

Hushai Helps David

2 Samuel 16:15–17:14

When Hushai, David's friend, got back to Jerusalem, Absalom and his followers were there. They had come back to Jerusalem while David and his people were fleeing from Jerusalem.

Hushai came to Absalom. He said, "God save the king! God save the king!"

Now Absalom knew that Hushai had been David's friend. Was Hushai only pretending to be his friend now by greeting him as king? Was he doing this so that he could show kindness to David? Absalom did not know. So he asked Hushai, "Is this the way you show kindness to your friend? Why did you not go along with your friend?"

Hushai answered, "No, I will stay with him whom the Lord and His people choose. As I have worked for your father, so will I work for you."

Absalom was not satisfied that Hushai would do as he said. But remember, Hushai was only pretending to be Absalom's friend so that he could help David. God had chosen David to be king, and Hushai would be faithful to him.

Absalom went to Ahithophel for advice. He said to Ahithophel, "Tell us what we shall do."

Ahithophel answered, "Let me now choose twelve thousand men, and I will go after David yet tonight. We will come to David when he is weak and tired and make him afraid. Then all the people who are with him will run away, and I will kill only the king. I will bring back all the people to you, and all the people will be contented."

This advice pleased Absalom and all the older men of Israel who were with him. They thought that Ahithophel's advice was very good.

Then Absalom said, "Call now Hushai, too. Let us listen also to what he has to say."

When Hushai came, Absalom told him what Ahithophel had advised him to do. He asked Hushai, "Shall we do as Ahithophel advised? If not, tell us."

Now Hushai knew that if they took Ahithophel's advice, he would not have time to send a message to David, warning him of what Absalom was planning to do. Ahithophel wanted to go after David to kill him yet that night.

So Hushai said to Absalom, "The advice that

Ahithophel has given is not good at this time. You know that your father and his men are mighty men. They are angry now like a bear when she is robbed of her cubs in the field. Your father is a man of war and will not stay with the people. Now he is hid in a pit or some other place. When his men kill some of your men, the rest of your men will be afraid. Even your valiant men who have hearts as the heart of a lion will be afraid. All Israel knows that your father is a mighty man, and all the men with him are mighty. Because of this, I advise you to gather all Israel to you from Dan even to Beer-sheba, as the sand that is by the seashore for numbers. You go along with them to battle. We will come to where David is and will light upon him as dew falls on the ground. Neither he nor any of his men shall be left alive."

Absalom and his men said, "The advice of Hushai is better than the advice of Ahithophel."

God caused the people to feel this way. God did not want them to take Ahithophel's advice and kill David. So God made Hushai's advice sound better to them than Ahithophel's advice. This way Hushai would have time to send a message to David to warn him of their plans. Then David could be saved and Absalom defeated.

God had heard and answered David's prayer. He had turned the advice of Ahithophel into foolishness.

Lesson 16

Absalom Goes After David

2 Samuel 17:15–18:5

Hushai went to the priests. He told them what advice Ahithophel had given to Absalom. He also told them what advice he had given. Then he said, "Now, because of this, send messengers quickly to David. Have them tell David not to stay in the plains of the desert tonight but to hurry and pass over the Jordan River."

Now the priests' sons were not allowed to be in Jerusalem. So a woman servant was sent to tell the priests' sons to go to David and tell him the news.

The priests' sons received the message and were soon on their way to go to David. But a young boy saw them go, and he went and told Absalom.

The priests' sons knew that they had been seen. They knew that it was not safe to continue on their journey. So they quickly went to a certain man's house along the way. In his yard was a well. The two sons of the priests quickly went down into this well to hide. The woman of the house spread a covering over the mouth of the well. Then she spread ground corn on the covering. This way the well could not be seen. It looked only as though the woman was drying ground corn in her yard.

Meanwhile Absalom had sent servants after the priests' sons. The servants came to the house of the woman who had hid the men. They asked the woman, "Where are the two sons of the priest?"

"They have gone over the brook of water," she said.

So the servants of Absalom went on after them. But, of course, they could not find them; so they finally went back to Jerusalem.

When it was safe, the two men came up out of the well. They went on to King David. They said to him, "Get up, and go quickly over the water."

It was nighttime, but David and all the people who were with him arose and went over the Jordan River. By the time it was light the next morning, all the people were across the river. They went to a nearby city.

While David was there, three men came to

him. They brought beds, basins, dishes, wheat, barley, corn, beans, flour, honey, butter, cheese, sheep, and other things that they thought David and his men might need. They knew that David and his men would be hungry, thirsty, and tired there in the desert. So they took pity on them and were very kind to them.

Meanwhile, Absalom and all the men of Israel who were with him got ready to do as Hushai had advised.

But when Ahithophel knew that King Absalom had not taken his advice, he was disappointed. He went back to his own city and to his own house. There he put his household in order. Then he hanged himself and died. He was buried in the grave of his father.

Since Joab, the captain of the army was with David, Absalom needed to make another captain. He chose Amasa for this job. Amasa was a first cousin to Joab. Both Joab's mother and Amasa's mother were sisters of David. After Amasa was made captain, Absalom and his men went after David. They went over the Jordan River and camped near the city where David was.

David prepared to go to battle against them. He counted his men and divided them into three groups. He made Joab captain over one group, Joab's brother Abishai captain over another group, and Ittai over one group. David said to the people, "I also will go along with you."

"You shall not go along," answered the people. "If we flee, Absalom and his men will not care. Neither will they care if half of us die. You are worth ten thousand of us."

King David said to them, "What seems best to you, I will do." So the king stood by the gate of the city. All the people came out by hundreds and thousands to go to battle against Absalom and his followers.

David commanded the three captains, "Deal gently with Absalom for my sake." All the people heard when David gave this command to the captains.

Lesson 17

A Great Battle

2 Samuel 18:6–33

David's men went out to fight against Absalom and his men. That day there was a great battle in the woods of Ephraim. Twenty thousand of Absalom's men were killed. More people were killed by the woods than by the sword. Absalom was riding on a mule when he met David's servants. As the mule went under the thick boughs of a great oak tree, Absalom's head caught in the oak. The mule went out from under Absalom. He was left hanging in the tree between the earth and the sky.

One of David's men saw what had happened. He said to Joab, "I saw Absalom hanging in an oak."

"Why did you not kill him if you saw him?" asked Joab. "I would have given you ten pieces of silver."

The man answered, "Though I would receive a thousand pieces of silver, I would not kill the king's son. In our hearing the king commanded you, your brother, and Ittai. He said, 'Beware that no one hurt the young man Absalom.' Nothing is hid from the king. Even you would have been against me if I had done this."

Joab then took three arrows in his hand. He thrust them into Absalom's heart while he was still alive in the tree. Then ten young men who were servants to Joab gathered around Absalom and killed him.

Joab blew the trumpet. The battle was over. All the people came back from going after their enemies.

David's men took Absalom down from the tree. They threw him into a big pit in the woods and laid a great pile of stones upon him.

When Absalom's followers saw that their leader was dead, they fled to their tents.

Zadok's son said to Joab, "Let me run now and bring news to the king that the Lord has destroyed his enemies."

Joab said to him, "You shall not take the news today. You shall take the news some other day. Today you shall not take the news because the king's son is dead."

Then Joab said to Cushi, "Go and tell the king what you have seen."

Cushi bowed before Joab, his captain. Then he ran to take news of the battle to David.

Zadok's son came to Joab again. He said, "Let me go and bring the king news. Let me also run after Cushi."

Joab asked, "Why will you run, my son, seeing that you do not have a message?"

But Zadok's son still begged, "Let me run."

So Joab said, "Run."

Zadok's son ran. He ran faster than Cushi and got ahead of him.

David sat between the two gates of the city. Watchmen were above him on the roof over the wall. They looked up and saw a man running all by himself. They said to David, "We see a man running. He is alone."

The king said, "If he is alone, he has news to tell us."

As the man came closer to the city, the watchmen looked again. Now they saw another man coming. The called to the gatekeeper below, "See, another man is running alone."

David said, "He is also bringing news."

The watchman said, "I think the first man runs the way Zadok's son runs."

David said, "Zadok's son is a good man. He

comes with good news."

Zadok's son called to David. He said, "All is well." He fell down on the ground before David and said, "Blessed be the Lord your God, who has delivered to us the men who were against you."

"Is the young man Absalom safe?" asked David.

Zadok's son answered, "When Joab sent me, I saw that there was a great commotion. But I did not know what it was all about."

"Step aside," said King David. So Zadok's son stepped over to the side and stood still.

Soon Cushi came. He said to David, "News, my lord, the king. The Lord has killed today of all those that rose up against you."

The king said to Cushi, "Is the young man Absalom safe?"

Cushi answered, "May your enemies and all those who tried to harm you be as that young man is."

David knew that these words meant that Absalom had been killed. He was much grieved because of this. He got up to go to his room over the gate and weep. As he was going, he cried out, "O Absalom, my son, my son Absalom! I wish that I could have died for you. O Absalom, my son, my son!" Then David went to his room and wept.

Absalom had been so wicked that he wanted to kill his father so that he could be king. Yet David's love for him was so great that he would have been willing to die in his place.

David Returns to Jerusalem

2 Samuel 19:1–30

The people were happy that God had given them the victory over their enemies. They rejoiced greatly. Then news came that King David was weeping for Absalom. When the people heard this, their joy quickly turned to sorrow.

The people sneaked back to the city. They acted as people do when they are ashamed because they have lost a battle.

The king covered his face. He cried with a loud voice, "O my son Absalom! O Absalom, my son, my son!"

Joab did not like the way King David was acting. He and his men had fought bravely to save David's life. Now David was crying instead of rejoicing. He did not seem thankful for what they had done.

Joab came to the king. He said, "You have shamed all your servants who have saved your life and your wives and sons and daughters. You shame them because you love your enemies and hate your friends. It looks to me as though you would be pleased if Absalom were still alive and we all would have died today. Now go and speak words of comfort to your servants. If you do not, not one of them will stay with you tonight. That will be worse for you than all the bad things that have happened to you from the time you were a young man until now."

King David got up and sat in the gate. The people were told, "The king sits in the gate."

Then all the people came before the king.

But King David was not pleased with Joab. Joab had not followed his orders about dealing gently with Absalom. David made Amasa, whom Absalom had made captain, to be captain in the place of Joab.

The other people of Israel who had followed Absalom now remembered what David had done for them in times past. They said, "The king saved us from our enemies. He delivered us out of the hand of the Philistines. Absalom, whom we anointed king, is dead in battle." Now ten tribes were ready to welcome David back as their king.

David could not understand why the ten tribes of Israel welcomed him back before his own tribe, the tribe of Judah. He asked the people of

Judah, "Why are you the last to bring me back to my house? You are my brethren."

Then all the tribe of Judah as one man gave David a warm welcome to come back to Jerusalem to be their king.

King David came to the Jordan river. There the tribe of Judah met him to bring him over the river. Shimei, the man who had cursed David and had thrown stones at him, hurried to come along with the men of Judah to meet David. He had with him a thousand men of the tribe of Benjamin. He also had with him Ziba and his fifteen sons and twenty servants. These all came to bring David over the Jordan River.

Barzillai also came down to the Jordan River. He lived on the opposite side of the river from where David lived in Jerusalem. He was a very great man. He was one of the men who had brought rich gifts to David and his men before the battle with Absalom. Now he wanted to help the king cross the river.

David appreciated his kindness very much. He wanted to do something for Barzillai. King David said to him, "Come over with me. I will feed you with me in Jerusalem."

Barzillai answered, "I am eighty years old

today. How much longer do I have to live that I should go along to Jerusalem with the king? Can I tell the difference between good and bad? Can I taste what I eat or what I drink? Can I hear any longer the voice of singing men and singing women? Why should I be a burden to the king? I will go a little way over Jordan with you. Why will you give me so much? Please let me go back again so that I can die in my own city and be buried in the grave of my father and my mother. Here is Chimham. Let him go over with the king. Do for him whatever seems good to you."

David answered, "Chimham shall go over with me. I will do for him whatever you desire. And whatever you ask me to do for you, I will do."

All the people and King David went over Jordan. There the king kissed Barzillai and blessed him. The Barzillai went back to his home, but Chimham went on with David.

A ferry went across the river to carry over for David whatever he wanted to bring back to Jerusalem.

The Tribes Quarrel

2 Samuel 19:31–20:2

When David came over Jordan, Shimei went and fell down before the king. He said, "Do not remember the wicked things that I did against you on the day that you went out of Jerusalem. I know that I have sinned. That is why I came first today of all the house of Joseph to meet you."

Joab's brother Abishai said to David, "Shall not Shimei be put to death because he cursed the man whom the Lord anointed king?"

But David was willing to forgive Shimei his great sin. He said to Shimei, "You shall not die."

At last David arrived back at his home in Jerusalem again. All the time that David had been gone, Mephibosheth had not bandaged his feet. He had not trimmed his beard, nor washed his clothes.

Now when the king came to Jerusalem in peace, Mephibosheth went to meet him.

King David said to him, "Why did you not go with me, Mephibosheth?"

Mephibosheth answered, "O King, my servant deceived me. For I said, 'I will saddle me a donkey that I may ride on it and go to the king because I am lame.' But my servant spoke the untruth about me. You are as an angel of God. Do whatever seems right to you because all my father's house were as dead men to you. Yet you set me among those who eat at your table. What right have I to beg anything more from you?"

David had told Ziba he could have Mephibosheth's land, but now he said to Mephibosheth, "You and Ziba divide the land." But Mephibosheth was willing to let Ziba have all the land. He was just very happy that David had returned safely to his own house.

Because David was of the tribe of Judah, the people of this tribe felt more closely related to David. Also, they felt more responsible to look after David. They had come to Jordan to bring the king, his wives, his children, and his servants back to Jerusalem.

This caused trouble between the men of Judah and the men of Israel. All the men of Israel came to David. They said, "Why have our brethren, the men of Judah, stolen you away? Why have they brought you and all the people who are with you over Jordan?"

The men of Judah answered the men of Israel for David. They said, "Because the king is a near relative of ours. Why are you angry about this? Have we eaten anything that the king paid for? Or has he given us any gift?"

The men of Israel answered, "We have ten parts in the king. We have more right in David than you do. Why then do you despise us? Why do you not let us first give our advice in bringing back the king?"

How sad that a quarrel should start so quickly again! One tribe thought they had more privileges in David because they were related to him. The ten tribes thought they had more privileges because they were ten tribes and Judah was only one. So they quarreled back and forth. The words of the men of Judah were fiercer than the words of the men of Israel.

A man of Belial heard the quarreling tribes. His name was Sheba, and he was of the tribe of Benjamin, the smallest of all the tribes. Sheba blew a trumpet and said, "We have no part in David. Neither do we have anything to receive from the son of Jesse. Every man to his tents, O Israel."

Every man of Israel then followed Sheba instead of David. Only the men of the tribe of Judah followed David.

The Quarrel Is Settled

2 Samuel 20:2–26

After the death of Absalom, David had made Amasa captain of his army in place of Joab. So now the king called Amasa to him. He wanted him to prepare to go to war against Sheba. He said, "Gather the men of Judah together. Be back within three days."

Amasa went to gather the men of Judah together for battle. But he stayed longer than he was told to stay. He was not back in three days as the king had commanded.

Now David was afraid that Sheba was doing more harm than Absalom had done. David told Joab's brother Abishai to take servants and go after Sheba and his followers. Joab's men and many other mighty men went out after Sheba. As they were going, they met Amasa at a great stone in Gibeon. The captain's clothes which Joab had worn were upon Amasa. As Amasa was traveling, the sword which was in its sheath upon his clothes fell out.

Joab saw the sword and picked it up. He came up to Amasa and asked, "How is your health, my brother?" He took Amasa by the beard with his right hand to kiss him. Amasa paid no attention to the sword that was in Joab's hand. Joab used the sword in his hand to kill Amasa. He left Amasa lying in the middle of the highway, and he and Abishai went on after Sheba. But the rest of the men did not follow them.

One of the men stood near to where Amasa lay. He said to the people, "If you are on Joab's side and on David's side, follow Joab."

Still the men stood still as they came to where Amasa lay in the highway. So the man took Amasa out of the highway into a field and threw a cloth over him. Then all the people followed after Joab to kill Sheba.

At last they came to Abel, the city in which Sheba was. Joab and all the people began beating on the wall of the city. They wanted to break down the wall so that they could get into the city.

A wise woman lived in the city of Abel. She cried out and said, "Listen! Listen! Please tell Joab, 'Come near that I may speak to you.'"

When Joab came near, the woman asked, "Are you Joab?"

Joab answered, "I am he."

The woman said, "Listen to the words of your handmaid."

"I am listening," said Joab.

The woman said, "I am peaceable and faithful in Israel. You are trying to destroy a city and a mother in Israel. Why will you destroy what belongs to the Lord?"

Joab answered, "Far be it, far be it from me that I should destroy. That is not the way it is. A man named Sheba has rebelled against King David. Give us only him, and we will leave the city."

The woman said to Joab, "His head shall be thrown to you over the wall."

Then the woman in all her wisdom talked to all the people of the city. They cut off the head of Sheba and threw it out to Joab.

Joah blew the trumpet, and they left the city. Each person went to his own tent, but Joab returned to the king at Jerusalem.

Once again Joab was made captain over David's army. He was a help to King David.

Israel Makes Things Right and Prospers

2 Samuel 21–24:1–9

For three years, one right after the other, there was a famine in the land of Israel. David went to the Lord to find out the reason for the famine.

The Lord said to David, "It is because Saul and his bloody men killed the Gibeonites."

Many years before, Israel had promised the Gibeonites that they would not destroy them. So Saul did wrong when he killed some of them.

David asked the Gibeonites, "What can we do to make things right with you that you will bless us?"

The Gibeonites answered, "We do not want gold or silver from Saul or his family. Neither shall you kill any man of Israel for us. But give to us seven sons of the man who said that we should be destroyed. We will hang them."

David said, "I will give them to you." So David gave the Gibeonites seven sons of Saul. But he did not let them have Mephibosheth, Jonathan's son, because of the agreement he had made with Jonathan. The Gibeonites hanged the seven sons of Saul on a hill. Then David gathered the bones of Saul and his sons that had been buried at Jabesh-gilead, and the bodies of the men who had been hanged. He buried them all in the land of Benjamin in the sepulcher of Saul's father. After this God blessed the land again.

The Philistines came again to fight against Israel. David and his servants went to battle against them. Among the Philistines was a son of a giant. He had a new spear and intended to kill David. But Joab's brother killed him, and David was not hurt. David was not able to defend himself. He had become weak and faint in the battle.

David's servants did not think that David should go to battle with them any more. He was getting older. He was not able to take much strain any more. They did not want David to be killed. They said to him, "You shall not go with us to battle any more."

There were many battles with the Philistines. In one battle, one of the giant's sons was killed. In another battle, a man from Bethlehem killed

Goliath's brother. There was still another battle in Gath, a city of the Philistines. In this battle was a very large man. He was the son of a giant. On each hand he had six fingers, and on each foot he had six toes. He came out against Israel as Goliath had done. David's nephew killed him.

Altogether Israel killed four sons of the giant. David was happy that the Lord had delivered Israel from their enemies. David sang a song to the Lord that day.

After this King David talked to Joab, the captain of his army. He said, "Go now through all the tribes of Israel. Number the people so that I can know how many there are."

Joab did not think that God would be pleased with this. God did not save Israel from their enemies because they were many people. He saved them because He loved them and they obeyed Him. Joab did not want to do what King David said. He protested to the king.

But King David insisted that the people be numbered. He wanted to know how many mighty men were in his kingdom. So Joab and his captains went throughout Israel to count the people. They were gone about ten months. It was a big job. But even in ten months they did not count all the people. Joab did not think it was right in God's sight to number all the people. Because of God's anger, he did not number the tribes of Levi and Benjamin. Of the people he did number, there were about one and one-half million men who were able to handle a spear and go to war.

At the end of nine months and twenty days, Joab and his captains came back to Jerusalem. They told King David how many men they had counted.

God Punishes Israel

2 Samuel 24:10–25; 1 Chronicles 21

After the men of Israel had been numbered, David felt miserable. He knew that he had done wrong in asking Joab to number Israel. David was sorry for his sin. He said to the Lord, "I have sinned greatly in what I have done. Now please, O Lord, take away the sin of Your servant; for I have done very foolishly."

In the morning after David got out of bed, God spoke to Gad the prophet. He said, "Go and say to David, 'This is what the Lord says, "I will offer you three things. Choose one of them so that I can do it to you." ' "

Gad came to David. He said, "The Lord says that you must choose one of these things. Shall seven years of famine come in your land? Or will you flee from your enemies for three months? Or shall there be three days of pestilence from the Lord when God's angel will destroy in Israel? Now tell me which you choose so that I can tell the Lord, who sent me."

David said to Gad, "I am in a great distress. I would rather fall into the hand of the Lord because His mercies are great. Let me not fall into the hand of man."

The Lord then sent a pestilence on Israel in the time that He said He would. Over seventy thousand people died of the disease. Finally the angel came to Jerusalem. He stretched out his hand upon Jerusalem to destroy it. But God said to the angel, "It is enough. Hold back your hand."

The angel of the Lord was standing by the threshing floor of a man named Ornan. David looked up. He saw the angel standing between heaven and earth with his sword stretched out over Jerusalem.

David and the older men of Israel fell upon their faces, clothed in sackcloth. David said to God, "Am I not the one who commanded Israel to be numbered? I am really the one who has sinned. But as for these sheep, what have they done? O Lord, please let Your punishment be on me and on my father's house, but not on Your people."

God's angel came to Gad the prophet. The angel said to Gad, "Tell David to set up an altar

to the Lord in the threshing floor of Ornan."

Now Ornan had been threshing wheat. But when he had seen the angel, he and his four sons had hid themselves. They were afraid.

Ornan saw King David coming to him. He came out of his hiding place and bowed himself to David with his face to the ground. He asked the king, "Why have you come to your servant?"

David said, "I have come to buy the threshing floor from you. I want to build an altar to the Lord here so that the plague on the people will stop."

Ornan said to David, "Let the king take whatever seems good to him and offer it. See, here are oxen for a burnt sacrifice, and there are threshing tools and other things." Ornan wanted to give all these things to the king.

But David said, "I must buy the things that I use. I must not offer to the Lord something that has not cost me anything." So David bought the threshing floor and the oxen for fifty pieces of silver.

David built an altar to the Lord there. On the altar he offered burnt offerings and peace offerings to the Lord. Then the Lord stopped the plague in Israel. No more people were killed by the angel.

David Plans a House for God

1 Chronicles 22

David had wanted to build a house for God. But God had told him that he should not build it. He had said that David's son Solomon would be the one to build the house.

Even though David could not build the house, he prepared for it before he died. He said, "Solomon my son is young and tender. The house that is to be built must be exceeding magnificent so that all the countries around us will know about it. I will prepare for it now."

David called for Solomon. He said to him, "You must build a house for the Lord God of Israel. My son, it was in my mind to build a house for the Lord God of Israel. But God came to me and said, 'You have shed much blood and have made great wars. You shall not build a house to My Name because you have shed much blood on the earth. A son shall be born to you who will be a man of peace. I will give him rest from his enemies round about. In his days, I will give peace and quietness to Israel. He shall build a house for My Name. He shall be My son, and I will be His Father. I will make his throne last forever.'

"Now, my son, the Lord be with you. Go on with the work and build the house of the Lord as He has said that you should do. The Lord give you wisdom and understanding so that you can keep God's laws. Be strong and of good courage. I, with much effort, have prepared for the house of the Lord. I have a hundred thousand talents of gold and a thousand thousand talents of silver.

"I have also more brass and iron than can be weighed because it is so much. I have also prepared timber and stone. And there are many workers. There are men who can cut stones. There are all kinds of workmen for all the different kinds of work. They are men who know how to do their work well. Arise, therefore, and go to work. The Lord be with you."

David talked to all the princes of Israel. He told them, "Help Solomon my son. Is not the Lord your God with you? Now set your heart and your soul to find out all that the Lord your God wants you to do. Arise and build the house of the Lord."

In the days of Moses, the children of Israel had built a tent for God's house. At that time they were traveling from Egypt to Canaan. It was wise for God's house to be in a tent while the children of Israel traveled from place to place. A tent could be taken down and carried when the people traveled. When they camped for a while, the tent could be set up and used.

When the children of Israel moved into Canaan, they had had many wars. They needed to drive out the people in the land of Canaan little by little. Even up until David's time there were many wars. This made it unsuitable to build a house for the Lord.

But now God had promised that when Solomon reigned as king, there would be no more wars. It would be a time of peace and rest. This would be a good time to build a house for God. This house would be called the temple. It would be built at Jerusalem, where the king lived.

Adonijah Wants to Be King

1 Kings 1:1–31

The time came when David was too old to look after the needs of the people in his kingdom. It was time for one of his sons to be made king in his place. God had chosen Solomon to take his place and be king after him.

Now David had many other sons besides Solomon. Many of his sons were older than Solomon. Adonijah was one of these older sons. He was next to Absalom in age. Absalom was David's third son, and Adonijah was his fourth son.

Adonijah was a spoiled son. His father had let him do what he wanted to do. He did not spank him when he was naughty. But Adonijah was a good-looking man. He seemed like a nice man. He decided to make himself a great man and be king. He said, "I will be king." Since he was used to having his own way, he thought he could be king if he wanted to be.

Adonijah talked to Joab and Abiathar the

priest. He told them of his desire to be king. They agreed to help him so that he could be king. But Zadok the priest, Nathan the prophet, and others of David's mighty men were not with Adonijah in his plans. They knew that it was not God's will that Adonijah should be king.

Adonijah prepared chariots, horsemen, and fifty men to run before him, just as Absalom had done. He killed sheep, oxen, and fat cattle. He called together all his brothers except Solomon, whom God had chosen to be king. Adonijah also called King David's servants and some of his mighty men.

Nathan the prophet came to Bath-sheba, Solomon's mother. He said, "Have you not heard that Adonijah is reigning and that David does not know it? Now please let me tell you what you should do to save your own life and the life of Solomon. Go to King David. Ask him, 'Did you not promise me that my son Solomon would reign and sit on your throne? Then why is Adonijah reigning?' While you are still talking to the king, I will also come. I will tell the king that what you are saying is true."

Bath-sheba did as Nathan the prophet said. She went into the king's bedroom. David was so old and feeble that he was in bed. Bath-sheba bowed to the king and showed him great respect.

King David asked her, "What would you like?"

Bath-sheba answered, "You promised me that my son Solomon would reign after you. You said that he would sit on your throne. Now Adonijah is reigning, and you do not know it. He has killed many oxen, fat cattle, and sheep. He has called all the king's sons, Abiathar the priest, and Joab the captain of your host to the celebration. But he has not called Solomon. Now the people of Israel are waiting for you to tell them who should be king after you. Otherwise, after you die, I and your son Solomon will be killed."

While Bath-sheba was still talking to David, Nathan the prophet came. Nathan bowed before the king. He said, "O king, have you said that Adonijah should reign after you and sit on your throne? He has gone today and killed many oxen, fat cattle, and sheep. He has called all the king's sons, the captains, and Abiathar the priest. They are feasting with him. They say, 'God save King Adonijah!' But he has not called Zadok the priest, Benaiah, Solomon, and me. Have you said that this should be done and did not tell us who should be king after you?"

The king answered, "Call Bath-sheba to me."

Bath-sheba came in and stood before the king. the king said to her, "As the Lord lives that delivered me out of all distress, Solomon will be king. I will see that he is made king yet today."

Bath-sheba bowed with her face to the ground. She said, "Let my lord King David live forever."

"God Save King Solomon!"

1 Kings 1:32–2:11

After King David had talked to Bath-sheba, he said, "Call Zadok the priest and Benaiah to me." Zadok and Benaiah came before the king. David said to them, "Take my servants with you. Have Solomon my son to ride on my own mule. Bring him down to Gihon. Then let Zadok the priest and Nathan the prophet anoint Solomon king over Israel. Blow with the trumpet and say, 'God save King Solomon!' Then bring him back to Jerusalem that he may sit upon my throne, for he shall be king in my place. I have appointed him to be ruler over Israel and Judah."

Benaiah answered the king, "Amen. Your Lord God says so also. As the Lord was with you, so let Him be with Solomon. Let Him make Solomon's throne greater than yours."

Zadok and Benaiah went out from the king. They did as David had commanded them. They had Solomon to ride on King David's mule. They brought him to Gihon, a place just outside of

Jerusalem. Zadok the priest took a horn of oil which he had taken from the tabernacle. He anointed Solomon to be king. They blew the trumpet, and all the people shouted, "God save King Solomon!" Many people followed King Solomon, piping on their pipes and rejoicing with great joy.

Adonijah and his guests were not far away. They had just finished eating when they heard the sound of rejoicing. When Joab heard the sound of the trumpet, he asked, "What does this noise mean?"

While Joab was still speaking, Jonathan, the son of Abiathar, came in. Adonijah said to him, "Come in, for you are a valiant man and bring good news."

Jonathan said to Adonijah, "King David has made Solomon king. They have anointed him king in Gihon. Now they are rejoicing. This is the noise that you have heard. And besides this, the king's servants came to bless King David. They say, 'God make Solomon's name better than your name. God make Solomon's throne greater than your throne.'"

When Adonijah's guests heard these things, they were afraid. They got up and ran away.

Adonijah was also afraid. He went and caught hold of the horns of the altar.

Someone came and told King Solomon, "Adonijah is afraid. He has gone and caught hold of the horns of the altar. He said, 'Let King Solomon promise me today that he will not kill me with the sword.'"

King Solomon answered, "If he shows himself worthy, not one of his hairs shall fall to the ground. But if wickedness is found in him, he shall surely die."

King Solomon called for Adonijah to come to him. The people brought him from the horns of the altar to King Solomon. Adonijah bowed himself before the king. Solomon said to him, "Go to your house." He meant that he should stay there.

David knew that he would soon die. He had some things he wanted to tell Solomon yet before he died. He called for Solomon to come to him. He said, "I am going the way of all the earth. Therefore be strong and show yourself a man. Do what the Lord tells you to do as He has written in the Law of Moses. Then everything you do will be right."

David died when he was seventy years old. He

had been king for forty years. He was buried in the city of David. Solomon, his son, reigned in his place.

Lesson 26

Solomon Prepares for
a Peaceable Reign

1 Kings 2:12–36

God blessed King Solomon exceedingly. And Solomon was careful to obey God so that He could keep on blessing him and the people of his kingdom. One of the first things King Solomon did was to punish the unworthy men in his kingdom. These were men who were not always faithful to David, his father.

First was Adonijah. He had risen up against David by trying to take the kingdom away from his son Solomon, whom God had chosen. Solomon did not want unfaithful men in his kingdom. They would not help to strengthen his kingdom. Solomon had said that Adonijah could live if he showed himself worthy. But Adonijah did not show himself worthy. So Solomon had him put to death.

Next Solomon spoked to Abiathar. He was the priest who had wanted to make Adonijah king instead of Solomon. Because of this, he too, was worthy to die. But Solomon did not kill him because he was God's priest and carried the ark of God and because he had been willing to suffer with David in his troubles. But Solomon would not let him be priest any longer. Abiathar was a great-great-grandson of Eli, who was the priest when Samuel was a boy. Solomon made Zadok priest in the place of Abiathar. Zadok had been faithful to God and to His servant David.

Joab, the captain of David's army, was also worthy to die. He had killed two men who were more righteous than he. And he had done it without David's permission. He had killed both Abner and Amasa, who were also captains. So Benaiah killed Joab as Solomon commanded him to do. Then Solomon made Benaiah captain in the place of Joab.

Next the king called for Shimei, the man who had cursed David. He said to Shimei, "Build a house at Jerusalem and live there. Do not leave the city to go anywhere. If you do leave the city and go over the brook Kidron, then know for sure that you will die."

Shimei said to the king, "What you say is good. As my lord the king has said, so will your servant do."

For many days Shimei stayed in Jerusalem. But at the end of three years, two of his servants ran away. Someone told Shimei, "Your servants are in Gath." Gath was a city in the land of the Philistines.

Shimei arose and saddled his donkey. He went to Gath to look for his servants. He found them there and brought them back to Jerusalem.

Someone told Solomon what had happened. Shimei had gone from Jerusalem to Gath and had come back again.

The king called for Shimei. He said, "Did I not tell you that on the day that you go out and go anywhere you shall surely die? And did you not say to me, 'What you have said is good?' Why then have you not kept the promise and the commandment that I gave you? You know all the wickedness that you did to David, my father. Because of this the Lord will return this wickedness to you. And King Solomon shall be blessed, and the throne of David shall continue before the Lord forever."

Then the king commanded Benaiah to kill Shimei. Now the enemies of David and Solomon were punished. Others would fear to be enemies to Solomon, whom God had chosen, knowing that they, too, would be punished. Solomon had done the work that needed to be done. Now God would bless his kingdom with peace.

God Gives Solomon Great Wisdom

1 Kings 3; 4; 1 Chronicles 1

Solomon loved the Lord and did as his father David had said that he should do. He went to Gibeon to offer a sacrifice to the Lord. He offered a thousand burnt offerings on the altar.

While Solomon was at Gibeon, God came to him in a dream at night. He said to Solomon, "Ask what I shall give you."

Solomon thought about God's mercy to David his father. He thought of His kindness in giving David a son to reign after him. But Solomon realized the great responsibility of the kingdom. He felt unable to direct the great nation of Israel. He said, "O Lord my God, You have made me king instead of my father, and I am just a little child. I do not know how I should rule. I am here among these people whom You have chosen. They are so many that they cannot be counted. Give me an understanding heart that I may know how to help these people and that I may know the difference between what is right and what is wrong."

The Lord was pleased that Solomon asked for wisdom to guide His people right. This was not a selfish request. God said to Solomon, "Because you have asked for this thing, and have not asked for riches for yourself or have not asked that your enemies should be killed, I have given you a wise and an understanding heart. There was never anyone like you before now. There will be no one like you after you are gone. I have also given you that for which you have not asked, both riches and honor, so that there will never be any other king like you. If you will obey Me as your father David did, I will let you live a long time."

Solomon awoke. He knew that the Lord had spoken to him in a dream. Solomon went back to Jerusalem and stood before the ark of God. There he offered burnt offerings and peace offerings. He made a feast to all of his servants.

Soon Solomon showed that he was a very wise king indeed. One day two women came to him for help. One of the women said, "O my lord, this woman and I live in the same house. I had a child born to me. Three days later this woman had a child born to her in the same house. No stranger was with us in the house. We two were alone. This woman's child died during the night because she lay on him. She got up at night and took my son from beside me while I was sleeping. She laid him beside her, and laid her dead child beside me. When I got up in the morning to feed my child, it was dead. But when I thought about it, I realized that it was not my son."

The other woman said, "No, the living child is my son, and the dead child is your son."

The woman who had spoken first said, "No, your son is the dead one, and mine is the living one."

Solomon needed to know which one was telling the truth. He said, "Bring me a sword." A sword was brought to the king. Then he said, "Divide the living child in two. Give half of it to the one woman and half to the other woman."

The woman who spoke the truth and was the mother of the living child loved her son. She did not want her child to be killed. She said to the king, "O my lord, let her have the living child. Do not kill it."

The other woman said, "Let it be neither hers nor mine, but divide it."

Now Solomon knew which was the mother. It was the one who truly loved the child and did not want it to be killed. He said, "Give her the living child. Do not kill him, for she is his mother."

Other wise men were living in the days of Solomon, but Solomon was wiser than the wisest of them. He was so wise that people in all the nations around him heard about him. He spoke three thousand wise sayings and sang one thousand five songs. Some of his wise sayings and songs are in the Bible. They are in the Book of Proverbs, Ecclesiastes, and Song of Solomon. We can read them and learn from them.

Solomon knew many things about trees, animals, birds, fishes, and insects. He talked about them. People came from all parts of the world to listen to him.

The Lord gave Solomon not only great wisdom, but also riches and honor. He had forty thousand stalls of horses and fourteen hundred chariots.

God had given the children of Israel a very wise king. All his days they lived in peace and safety.

Lesson 28

Solomon Builds the Temple

1 Kings 5:1–7:51; 2 Chronicles 2–5

In the northwest part of the land of Israel, along the coast of the Great Sea, was a country which Israel had never conquered. In this land were the famous mountains of Lebanon. Great trees of cedar, fir, and algum grew in these mountains. On the seacoast of this land was a famous city called Tyre. In the days of David and Solomon, Hiram was the king of this city. He had always loved David. When he heard that Solomon was king in David's place, he sent his servants to Solomon.

Solomon sent the following message back to Hiram. "You know that my father David could not build a house to the Name of the Lord his God because of the wars around him on every side. Now the Lord has given me peace on every side. I have no enemies, and no evil things are happening to me. I plan to build a house to the Name of the Lord my God, as the Lord told David my father. The Lord said, 'Your son, whom I have set upon your throne in your place, shall build a house to My Name.' Now send me a man who can work well in gold, silver, brass, and iron. I want him to work with my men. Send me also cedar trees, fir trees, and algum trees out of Lebanon because I know that none of my servants can cut down trees as your servants can. My servants will also work with your servants. They will prepare me timbers in abundance because the house which I am about to build shall be great and magnificent. I will pay your servants whatever you ask."

Hiram was very happy to get this message from Solomon. He said, "Blessed be the Lord this day who has given David a wise son over this great people."

Hiram wrote a letter to Solomon. In the letter he said, "I have considered the message you sent to me. I will do what you want about the fir and cedar timber. My servants will cut as many trees as you need. They will bring them down from Lebanon to the sea. I will send them in floats to Joppa. You can receive them there. For wages you can give me food for my household."

King Solomon was thankful for this message. He got ready thirty thousand men for the great work of getting the trees from Lebanon. Each month he sent ten thousand men to Lebanon. After they had worked a month, they could come home again and be at home for two months. When one group came home, another group of ten thousand men went to Lebanon. After two months at home, each group went back to work for one month again. This continued until there was enough timber to build the house of God.

Solomon needed men besides those who worked in the timber. He needed men to get stones ready for the foundation of the temple. He had eighty thousand men to cut the stones in the mountains. He had seventy thousand men to carry the stones. Many of the stones were large and very costly. Besides all the workmen to cut and carry stones, Solomon had appointed more than three thousand men to be rulers over the people. They told the workmen what to do. There was much work to do, and many workmen were needed. The temple was to be great because the people had a great God.

At last the work of preparing materials for the temple was finished. The stones had been cut and carried. The timber had been brought from Lebanon. Now it was time to begin the great work of building the temple. This work began in the fourth year after Solomon was anointed king over Israel. It began four hundred eighty years after the children of Israel left the land of Egypt. Even though Solomon had thousands of workmen, it took seven years to build the temple. Truly it was a great task.

Much noise is usually heard when men are building a house. Hammers pound noisily. Saws buzz. But no hammer, no ax, and no iron tool was heard while the temple was being built. The temple went up quietly. The stones had been made ready before they were brought.

The walls, ceiling, and floor of the temple were made of cedar wood and fir wood. All the wood was covered with gold. The temple was arranged very much like the tabernacle. The front part of the temple was made into a separate room for a place in which to set the ark of God. But the temple was much larger than the tabernacle had been. It was also much more costly and magnificent. It had extra rooms and porches.

A sea was made for the priests to wash in. Metal was heated and put into a mold to make a large container for the sea. It held about twenty thousand gallons of water. This sea stood on the images of twelve oxen. Three oxen looked toward the north, three toward the west, three toward the south, and three toward the east.

In the temple were beautiful carvings. There were carvings of fruits, flowers, palm trees, and cherubims.

This beautiful temple stood at Jerusalem in Mount Moriah, the place David had prepared for it.

Solomon's Glorious Reign

1 Kings 8:1–10:29; 2 Chronicles 6:9–28

After a time of preparation and seven years of building, the temple was finished. At last it was ready to use. Solomon called for the older men of Israel and for the heads of the tribes. He told them to bring the ark of God and set it in the most holy place in the temple. All the older men of Israel came, and the priests brought the ark into the temple. A great congregation of people had met at the temple. There was much singing and great rejoicing.

When the priests came out of the holy place, a cloud filled the house of the Lord. Because the glory of God filled the house, the priests could not do their work.

King Solomon blessed all the congregation of Israel while the people stood. Solomon stood before the altar in the presence of all the people. He stretched out his hands, kneeled down, and prayed to God. When he had finished praying, he stood and blessed the people again. Then fire came down from heaven. It burned up the burnt offering and sacrifices. The glory of God filled the house.

When the people saw this, they bowed themselves with their faces to the ground. They worshiped the Lord, saying, "For He is good. For His mercy endures forever."

Solomon offered to the Lord a sacrifice of twenty-two thousand oxen and one hundred twenty thousand sheep. Solomon and the people dedicated the house to the Lord. They had a feast for seven days.

Besides the first feast of seven days, they held also another feast for seven days. This last feast was called the Feast of Tabernacles. The children of Israel kept this feast in the seventh month of the year. So altogether they feasted fourteen days. Then on the fifteenth day, there was a solemn meeting. The people sacrificed so many sheep and oxen that they could not be counted.

When Solomon sent the people away, they blessed the king. Then they went home to their tents, joyful and glad in their hearts. They were thankful for what the Lord had done for them.

After this the Lord appeared to Solomon in the night. He said to Solomon, "I have heard your prayer that you have made before Me. I have made this house which you have built holy to put My Name there forever. My eyes and My heart shall be there all the time. If you obey Me as David your father did, then I will establish your kingdom forever. But if you or your children do not keep My laws, but go and serve other gods and worship them, then I will cut off Israel out of this land. And this house which I have made holy will I cast out of My sight. Then people shall ask, 'Why has the Lord done this to this land and to this house?' And the answer will be, 'Because they forsook the Lord their God. That is why the Lord has brought this evil upon them.' "

Besides building the temple, Solomon spent thirteen years in building a house for himself. He built this house also of the forest of Lebanon. He built many cities.

Far from Jerusalem, in a country called Sheba, lived a queen who heard about the wisdom of Solomon. She wanted to visit him and ask him hard questions to see how wise he really was.

The Queen of Sheba came to King Solomon with a large company of people. She came with camels that carried spices and huge amounts of gold and precious stones. She asked Solomon hard questions, but there was not one question that he could not answer. The Queen of Sheba saw that King Solomon was very wise.

The queen saw the magnificent house that Solomon had built. She saw how many people ate at his table and how much food was provided for them each day. There were about one hundred barrels of fine flour, and twice that much coarse flour, or meal. There were ten fat oxen, besides twenty oxen out of the pasture. Then there were a hundred sheep, besides deer and fat birds. All this was food for only one day. The queen saw how Solomon's servants were dressed and how they waited on him. She was astonished. She had never seen anything like it. She said to the king, "What I heard in my own land about your work and your wisdom was true. But I did not believe what I heard until I came and saw it with my own eyes. They did not tell me even half of it. Your wisdom and riches are much greater than what I had heard. Happy are your men and your servants who stand before you and hear your wisdom. Blessed be the Lord your God who delighted in you to set you on the throne of Israel. It is because the Lord loved Israel forever that He made you king to do what is right."

The Queen of Sheba gave Solomon many spices, precious stones, and much gold. She, too, was very rich. Yet Solomon's riches were so much greater than hers that she could hardly believe her eyes.

Solomon also gave gifts to the Queen of Sheba. He gave her whatever she asked of him. Then she and her servants went home to their own land.

King Solomon had many ships. Once every three years these ships came in. They brought gold, silver, ivory, apes, and peacocks.

People from everywhere came to Solomon to hear the wisdom which God had put into his heart. When they came, they brought him gifts. Truly God had given Solomon riches, honor, and wisdom.

Lesson 30

A Very Sad End

1 Kings 11

Solomon's reign was indeed a most glorious time in all the history of Israel. When Israel was in Egypt, they suffered greatly from hard work and mean treatment. In the forty years that they traveled in the wilderness from Egypt to Canaan, they often complained and had to be punished. In the four hundred forty years that they lived in Canaan there were many wars to be fought. Now four hundred eighty years after they came out of Egypt the people enjoyed a time of peace and plenty. They had a wise king who could teach them many good things. They had a great temple in which they could worship the Lord.

But, alas, Solomon failed to obey all of God's laws. In the Law of Moses, God had given a special commandment to kings. It said, "He shall not have many wives so that he turns away from Me." Altogether Solomon had seven hundred wives which were princesses, besides three hundred other women. Solomon loved his wives, but many of his wives did not love the true God. God does not want His people to have wives who do not love Him. They lead their husbands to worship their gods.

This is just what happened to Solomon. When he was old, his wives turned his heart away from the true God to their gods. Solomon even built places for his wives to worship their gods.

The Lord was angry with Solomon for this. The Lord had blessed Solomon in very special ways. He had warned him not to go after other gods. Solomon did not obey the Lord in this. God cannot bless people in their sins.

The Lord said to Solomon, "Because you have not obeyed Me, I will take the kingdom away from you and will give it to your servant. For your father David's sake, I will not take the kingdom away in your days. I will take it away in the days of your son. And for David's sake and for the sake of Jerusalem, I will not take away all the kingdom, but will give one tribe to your son."

After this, the Lord raised up people to be enemies to Solomon. They stirred up trouble for him. Even one of his servants became his enemy. He was Jeroboam, the son of a widow woman. Jeroboam was a mighty man and very industrious. Solomon saw this and made him to be one of his rulers.

One time Jeroboam went out of Jerusalem wearing a new garment. Ahijah the prophet of God found him. While they were alone in the field, Ahijah caught hold of Jeroboam's new garment. He tore it into twelve pieces. He said to Jeroboam, "You take ten pieces because the Lord said that He will take the kingdom away from Solomon and give ten tribes to you. He will keep one tribe for David's sake and for the sake of Jerusalem. Because Israel has forsaken the Lord and has gone after other gods, God will take the kingdom from Solomon's son. He will give you ten tribes. If you will obey the Lord, He will be with you and give Israel to you."

Solomon did not want Jeroboam to be king after him. He wanted his own son Rehoboam to be king. So he tried to kill Jeroboam. Because of this, Jeroboam fled to Egypt. He stayed there until after Solomon was dead.

Solomon reigned as king in Jerusalem for forty years. When he died, he was buried in the city of David. Rehoboam his son was made king over Israel. But this did not change what God had said. His word always comes to pass.

Unit Two

Stories of the Kings—
Rehoboam to Jehoram

The Kingdom Divides

1 Kings 12:1–24

Rehoboam went to Shechem. The people of Israel had gathered there to make him king.

In Egypt, Jeroboam heard that Solomon was dead and that Rehoboam had been made king. When he heard this, he left Egypt and came back to the land of Israel.

The people of Israel sent and called for Jeroboam. Together the men of Israel and Jeroboam went to the new king. They said to King Rehoboam, "Your father made us work too hard. Now if you will not make us work so hard, we will serve you."

Rehoboam was young. He was not sure how he wanted to rule the people. He wanted time to think about what the people had said. He said to them, "You leave and come back to me after three days."

The people left. For three days, they waited. Meanwhile, Rehoboam went to get advice on how to answer the people when they returned. First he called for the older men. They had been with his father, Solomon, while he was still living. They had learned from his wisdom. They had also learned from his mistakes. They gave good advice. They told Rehoboam, "If you will be a servant to these people and speak kindly to them, they will always serve you."

Sad to say, Rehoboam did not take the good advice of the older men. He called for the young men who grew up with him. He said, "What advice do you give to answer these people who spoke to me and asked me to make their work easier?"

These young men told him to say, "My father made you work hard, but I will make you work harder. My father punished you with whips, but I will punish you with scorpions."

On the third day Jeroboam and all the people came back to Rehoboam. They wanted to hear how Rehoboam would rule them. Rehoboam spoke roughly to them. He said, "My father gave you much work to do, but I will give you more work. My father punished you with whips, but I will punish you with scorpions."

The people saw that Rehoboam could not be persuaded to be a kind ruler. Most of the people

decided that they would not let Rehoboam rule over them. Only the tribe of Judah and the people who lived in their cities stayed with Rehoboam. This included the small tribe of Benjamin. The other ten tribes made Jeroboam their king and followed him. It was just as the prophet Ahijah had said.

Rehoboam sent out one of his officers who had charge of the tax money. The people of Israel stoned him with stones, and he died. This frightened Rehoboam. He hurried to his chariot to escape and go to Jerusalem. At Jerusalem he got his army ready to go and fight against the ten tribes of Israel. He was going to force them to let him be king over them.

God spoke to Shemaiah, the man of God. He said, "Tell Rehoboam and the people who are with him that the Lord says they are not supposed to go and fight against their brothers."

The king and the people listened to Shemaiah as he told them what God had said. They returned home instead of going to fight against Israel.

The kingdom of Israel was now two kingdoms. King Saul, Israel's first king, had reigned over all Israel for forty years. King David and his son Solomon also had reigned over all the tribes of

Israel. But from the days of Rehoboam, Israel and Judah were always separate kingdoms. Israel had her own kings, and the tribe of Judah had her own kings. Judah's kings were always of the house of David.

The kingdom of Israel and the kingdom of Judah each had their own capital city. The capital city was the city where the king lived. Jerusalem was the capital city of Judah, and Samaria was the capital city of Israel. Samaria was north of Jerusalem. For this reason, the kingdom of Israel is sometimes called the Northern Kingdom, and the kingdom of Judah the Southern Kingdom.

Jeroboam Causes Israel to Sin

1 Kings 12:25–33; 14:21–31

The Lord had said to Jeroboam, "If you obey Me, I will be with you. I will build you a sure house as I built for David." But Jeroboam did not trust the Lord. He was afraid that sometime the ten tribes would leave him and join themselves to Rehoboam. He said to himself, "If my people go up to sacrifice to the Lord at Jerusalem, they will want to go back to Rehoboam. They will kill me and go back to him." To keep this from happening, Jeroboam thought of a way to keep his people from going to Jerusalem to worship at the temple. He made two calves of gold. He said to the people of Israel, "You have gone up long enough to Jerusalem to worship. See your gods, O Israel, which brought you up out of the land of Egypt."

Jeroboam set one of the calves at Bethel, which was at the southern end of his kingdom. He put the other one at Dan, which was at the northern end of his kingdom. The people went to worship before these idols. This became a sin to them.

When people start to sin, they sin more and more. God had said that only men of the tribe of Levi were to be priests. But Jeroboam did not use the Levites for priests. He made anyone a priest. At Bethel he had the people hold a feast very much like the one that the people of Judah kept. The people of Judah kept the Feast of Tabernacles in the seventh month, as God had commanded. But Jeroboam had his people keep the feast in the eighth month, according to his own choosing. At the feast they offered sacrifices to the calves which he had made, and Jeroboam burned incense. This was a very wicked thing to do, for not only did Jeroboam sin, but he caused the people of Israel to sin. He is known as "Jeroboam the son of Nebat, who made Israel to sin."

Not all the Israelites followed Jeroboam in his idol worship. The priests and the Levites wanted to be faithful to the Lord. They were willing to leave all they had to go to Jerusalem and serve the Lord. There were other people who still wanted to serve the Lord. When the Levites went back to the kingdom of Judah, these people went along with them. They made the kingdom of

Judah a stronger kingdom.

For three years Rehoboam and the people walked in the ways of David and Solomon. As long as Rehoboam served the Lord, he was a strong king. But Rehoboam fell into the sin of his father Solomon. He wanted many wives. After three years, Rehoboam and all the people with him disobeyed the Lord. Because of this, God was going to punish them.

In the fifth year that Rehoboam was king, God used the king of Egypt to punish him. He came up and fought against Jerusalem. His army was huge. There were twelve hundred chariots and sixty thousand men who rode on horses. Besides these horsemen, there were so many other people that they could not even be numbered. But nothing is too hard for the Lord. God could have destroyed them. But He did not, because Judah had forsaken the Lord. They could not overcome their enemies. The king of Egypt came and took many of Judah's cities away from them. He even came to Jerusalem, intending to take it also.

Shemaiah the prophet went to Rehoboam and to his princes. He said, "The Lord says that because you have forsaken Him, He will give you to the king of Egypt."

This helped Rehoboam to see how helpless he was without the Lord. When he and the princes heard what Shemaiah said, they humbled themselves. They said, "The Lord is righteous."

The Lord saw that they humbled themselves. He saw that they realized God's punishment to them was what they deserved. They did not deserve His help. They deserved to be given to the king of Egypt because they had disobeyed God. Now because they humbled themselves, God could show mercy to them. He said to the prophet Shemaiah, "They have humbled themselves. I will not destroy them, but they will be servants to the king of Egypt."

The Lord still let the king of Egypt come up against Jerusalem. He took away all the treasures from the temple and from the king's house. This included the three hundred shields of gold which Solomon had made. Each of these shields had three pounds of gold. But, though Judah lost many things, God was merciful and true to His promise. He did not let the king of Egypt destroy the people. Later Rehoboam made shields of brass to take the place of the golden shields that were taken.

For seventeen years Rehoboam reigned over

Judah. All his days there was war between him and Jeroboam. Rehoboam died when he was fifty-eight years old. He was buried in the city of David.

A Man of God Comes to Bethel

1 Kings 13:1–13

One day Jeroboam, king of Israel, was standing by the altar at Bethel, burning incense. While he stood there, a man of God from the kingdom of Judah came to him. God had told him to come and speak against the altar. The man of God said, "O altar, altar, this is what the Lord says: 'Behold, a child shall be born to the house of David. His name shall be Josiah. On you he shall offer the priests that burn incense on you, and men's bones shall be burned on you.'"

The Lord also gave a sign so they would know that what the man of God said was truly the word of the Lord. He said, "This is the sign by which you can know that what the man of God said is true. The altar shall be torn apart, and the ashes that are upon it shall be poured out."

King Jeroboam did not like what the man of God said against the altar. It was not good news to hear that a king of Judah would burn their priests on these altars he had set up. He wanted to get rid of this man of God. He reached out his hand and said, "Get him." But the hand which he reached out against the man of God dried up. He could not use it. He could not even bring it back to himself again.

Then the sign that the Lord had given the man of God happened. The altar was torn apart. The ashes on the altar poured out. King Jeroboam knew that what the man of God had said was truly the word of the Lord. He was afraid. He said to the man of God, "Please talk to the Lord for me. Pray for me that He may restore my hand."

The man of God prayed for King Jeroboam. The Lord was merciful and restored his hand. His withered hand was well, and he could use it again.

Now King Jeroboam was ready to be kind to the man of God. He said, "Come home with me and refresh yourself. I will give you a reward."

But the man of God answered, "If you give me half your house, I will not go with you. Neither will I eat bread nor drink water in this place. This is because the Lord told me not to eat any bread nor drink any water here. He also told me not to return home the same way that I came."

The man of God started on his journey homeward. He did not go back the same way that he had come to Bethel. He wanted to obey God.

At Bethel there lived an old prophet. His sons
came home and told him what the man of God had
done at Bethel that day. They told him what the
man had said when the king invited him to come
to his house.

"Which way did he go?" asked their father.
His sons had seen which way the man of God had
gone, and they told their father which way he
went. The old prophet wanted to go and talk to
this man of God. He said to his sons, "Saddle the
donkey for me."

The sons saddled their father's donkey, and
the old prophet rode after the man of God.

Lesson 4

The Disobedient Prophet

1 Kings 13:14–34

The old prophet from Bethel found the man of God sitting under an oak tree. He said, "Are you the man of God who came out of Judah?"

"I am," answered the man of God.

The old prophet said, "Come home with me and eat bread."

"I cannot come home with you," answered the man of God. "Neither can I eat bread nor drink water in this place. The Lord told me not to eat any bread nor drink any water in this place, nor to go home the same way that I came."

The old prophet answered, "I am a prophet as you are. An angel talked to me. He told me that God said I should bring you back with me to my house so that you can eat with me." The old prophet lied to the man of God. An angel had not spoken to him. But the man of God believed what the old prophet said. He went back with the old prophet. He ate bread and drank water with him. This was disobedience to what God had plainly told him.

The man of God and the old prophet were sitting at the table when God spoke to the old prophet. Then the old prophet told the man of God what the Lord said. He said, "God says that because you have not obeyed the Lord, you will die before you reach home. And you will not be buried in the grave where your fathers are buried."

When they had finished eating, the old man saddled the donkey for the man of God. Then the man of God started for home. On the way, a lion met him and killed him. His dead body lay in the path. The donkey and the lion both stood by the dead body.

Some men passed by and saw the dead body lying in the way. When they came to Bethel, they told the people in the city what they had seen.

The old prophet heard about this. He said, "It is the man of God who was disobedient to what the Lord said. It is because he was disobedient that the Lord allowed the lion to kill him."

The old prophet said to his sons, "Saddle the donkey for me." Then he went on his donkey to find the man of God. He found his dead body lying in the path. The donkey and the lion were standing by the body. The lion had not eaten the dead body nor hurt the donkey. This was very unusual. But the Lord had kept the lion from doing it.

The old prophet took the dead body of the man of God. He laid it upon his donkey. He brought him back to the city to mourn for him and to bury him. He put the body in his own grave. The people mourned for him, saying, "Alas, my brother!"

After the old prophet had buried the man of God, he said to his sons, "When I am dead, bury me in the grave where the man of God is buried. Lay my bones beside his bones, because all that he said would happen will surely come to pass."

Lesson 5

Sad News

1 Kings 14:1–18

Even after the man of God had prophesied against the altar, Jeroboam did not take warning. He did not turn from his sinful ways. He still disobeyed God's laws. He still made priests of men who were not Levites. He even made himself a priest. This thing became a sin to the house of Jeroboam. The Lord was going to destroy him.

At that time Abijah, the son of Jeroboam, became sick. Jeroboam wanted to know if his son would get well or if he would die. He believed that Ahijah the prophet could tell him. Ahijah was the one who had told him that he would be king over Israel. This had come to pass as Ahijah had said. But Jeroboam did not go to Ahijah himself. Perhaps he was ashamed to go because he had disobeyed the Lord. He sent his wife to Ahijah to find out if the child would live or die.

Jeroboam did not even want Ahijah to know that his wife came to him. He said to her, "Please disguise yourself so no one will know that you are my wife. Go to Shiloh. The prophet Ahijah, who told me that I would be king over these people, is there. Take ten loaves, some cakes, and a bottle of honey with you. He will tell you what will become of the child."

Jeroboam's wife did as her husband said. She disguised herself so people would not know who she was. Then she went to the house of Ahijah at Shiloh.

Ahijah was old and blind. It made no difference how the wife of Jeroboam looked. He could not see her anyway. But she could not fool him. The Lord had told Ahijah that she was coming. He said, "The wife of Jeroboam is coming to ask you about her son because he is sick. When she comes she will pretend to be another woman." The Lord also told Ahijah what to tell her when she came.

As the wife of Jeroboam came in at the door, Ahijah heard the sound of her feet. He called to her and said, "Come in, wife of Jeroboam. Why are you pretending to be another woman?"

How surprised she must have been! But Ahijah went on talking to her. He said, "I am sent to you with sad news. Go and tell Jeroboam what the Lord says. This is what He says: 'I have made you a great man from among the people. I have made you prince over my people Israel. I took the kingdom away from the house of David and gave it to you. Yet you have not been like David. He kept My commandments. He followed Me with all his heart to do only what is right. But you have done more evil than anyone before you because you have made other gods to provoke me to anger. You would not have anything to do with Me. Because of this I will bring evil on your house. I will not have anything to do with you and your house. The men of your house who die in the city, the dogs will eat. The men who die in the field, the birds of the air will eat.'"

Then Ahijah told Jeroboam's wife, "Now get up and go to your own house. When your feet enter the city, the child will die. All Israel shall mourn for him and bury him. He is the only one of Jeroboam's children who will be put in a grave, because the Lord sees some good in him.

"Besides this, the Lord will raise up a king over Israel who will destroy the house of Jeroboam. He will take Israel out of this good land that He gave to their fathers. He will scatter them beyond the river because they provoked the Lord to anger. He will forsake Israel because of the sins of Jeroboam, who sinned and caused Israel to sin."

This was much sad news for the wife of Jeroboam. She got up and went home. When she came to the door of her house, the child died. They buried him, and all Israel mourned for him. Everything happened as the Lord had said by Ahijah the prophet.

Lesson 6

Israel Disobeys

1 Kings 14:19–16:6; 2 Chronicles 13

Jeroboam and Rehoboam each had a son named Abijah. Jeroboam's son Abijah was the one who had become sick and died. After Jeroboam had been king for about eighteen years, Abijah the son of Rehoboam became king of Judah. All the days that his father Rehoboam had been king, there was war between Jeroboam and Rehoboam. Now there was war between Jeroboam and Rehoboam's son Abijah.

Abijah tried to persuade Jeroboam and his people not to fight with them. He said, "Listen to me, Jeroboam and Israel. Should you not know that God gave the kingdom to David and to his sons? Yet Jeroboam has rebelled against Rehoboam. When Rehoboam was young and tenderhearted and could not stand against them, they worked against him. Now you are trying to work against the Lord. You are a great multitude of people. With you there are golden calves which Jeroboam made to be your gods. Have you not gotten rid of the priests of the Lord, the sons of Aaron and the Levites? Have you not made you priests as other nations do? But as for us, the Lord is our God. We have not forsaken Him. The priests which do the Lord's work are the sons of Aaron, and the Levites do their business. They burn sacrifices and sweet incense to the Lord every morning and every evening. They also set the shewbread upon the pure table and the candlestick of gold with the lamps to burn every evening. We obey the Lord our God. But you have forsaken Him. God is with us to be our captain. O children of Israel, do not fight against the Lord God of your fathers; for if you do, it will not be well with you."

Israel would not listen. Jeroboam came up against Judah with his army. They came up behind them and also in front of them. The people of Judah saw the battle in front of them. They looked behind them and saw the battle behind them, too. They did not know what to do nor which way to go. But they did what all of God's people should do at such a time. They called upon the Lord to help them. Then the priests blew the trumpets and the men of Judah shouted. When they shouted, the Lord helped them. King Abijah and his men were able to kill so many men of Israel that the rest ran away from before Judah. Five hundred thousand men of Israel were killed. Judah also captured many of their towns. From that time on Jeroboam was not able to come up against Judah in battle. This was because the people of Judah called upon God and put their trust in Him.

King Abijah became a mighty man. But Abijah's heart was not perfect before God. Altogether he had fourteen wives and twenty-two sons and sixteen daughters. He did not live very long. After he was king for about three years, he died. His son Asa became king in his place.

Two years after Asa became king of Judah, the Lord struck Jeroboam, king of Israel; and he died. His son, Nadab, became king after him. Nadab did the sinful things that his father Jeroboam had done. God could not bless him. About two years after he became king, Baasha, a man of another tribe, killed Nadab and became king in his place.

When Baasha was king, he killed all the people of the house of Jeroboam. The word of the Lord that Ahijah the prophet had spoken had come to pass. The Lord punished Jeroboam for his sin and for causing the people of Israel to sin.

But Baasha was also a wicked king. He also did the sinful things that Jeroboam had done. Because of this, God said, "I will destroy your house as I have destroyed the house of Jeroboam."

Good King Asa

1 Kings 15:9–24; 2 Chronicles 14:1–17:1

Asa, the son of Abijah, was a good king. For ten years after he became king the people of Judah enjoyed quietness in their land. Asa broke the idols that his father had made. He took away the altars of the strange gods. He commanded the people of Judah to come back to the God of their fathers and obey Him. Asa would not even let his mother be queen any longer, because she had made an idol in a grove. Asa burned her idol. Asa's heart was perfect before God all his life.

God richly blessed Asa, king of Judah, because he trusted God and obeyed Him. Even when an enemy came against him with a million people, he did not become frightened. He knew that the Lord could help him no matter how many people there were. He called on the Lord for help. Then Judah was able to overcome their enemies and take many valuable things from them.

After the battle, one of God's prophets went out to meet King Asa. He said, "Listen to me,

Asa, and all Judah and Benjamin. The Lord is with you while you obey Him. But if you forsake Him, He will forsake you. Now for a long time Israel has been without the true God. They have been without a priest to teach them. They have been without law. But when they were in trouble, and turned to the Lord, God helped them. When their enemies came out to destroy them, God destroyed their enemies. Be strong. Do not let you hands be weak, because your work shall be rewarded."

These words from God's prophet gave Asa much courage to be true to God. He destroyed the idols in Judah and Benjamin and set up the altar of the Lord. When the people of other tribes saw that the Lord was with Asa, some of them came over to his kingdom. They and Judah and Benjamin together offered to the Lord seven hundred oxen and seven thousand sheep. They made up their minds to serve the Lord with all their hearts and souls. They decided to put to death anyone who would not obey the Lord. All the people of Judah rejoiced because they said that they wanted to serve the Lord, and they meant what they said.

After this Baasha, king of Israel, came up to

fight against Judah. Asa called upon the king of Syria to help him fight against Israel. This did not please God. The king of Syria was a heathen king. A heathen king does not know God and obey Him. God sent a prophet to Asa to help him to see that he had done wrong. He should have called upon the Lord, the King of all the earth, for help as he had done before.

The prophet said to Asa, "Because you have trusted in the king of Syria and have not trusted in the Lord your God, the armies of the king of Syria have escaped from you." The prophet reminded Asa of the time a million people had come to fight against him. He said, "Yet, because you trusted in the Lord, He helped you to overcome them. For the eyes of the Lord run to and fro throughout the whole earth to show Himself strong in behalf of those whose hearts are perfect toward Him. You have done foolishly in this thing. Because of this, you will have wars from now on."

Asa did not like this message of the prophet. He was so angry with him that he put him into prison.

The Lord caused Asa to get a very serious disease in his feet. Instead of going to the Lord for help, Asa went to doctors. But the doctors could not cure his disease. Two years after Asa got the disease, he died. He had been king for nearly forty-one years. He was buried in the grave that he had made for himself in the city of David. Jehoshaphat his son reigned as king in his place.

During the time Asa was king of Judah, seven different kings reigned over Israel. They were Jeroboam (who was the first king of Israel), Nadab, Baasha, Elah, Zimri, Omri, and Ahab. Not one of them was a good king. In fact, the last two of these kings did more evil than the wicked kings before them. Ahab did more to provoke the Lord to anger than all the kings who lived before him. He did not think it was enough wickedness just to do the wicked things that Jeroboam had done. Besides this, he took a heathen princess to be his wife. She was a very wicked woman. Her name was Jezebel. Ahab and Jezebel set up an altar for a god called Baal and worshiped there.

God Cares for Elijah

1 Kings 17

When wicked Ahab was king, a good prophet lived in Israel. His name was Elijah. The Lord sent him to King Ahab with a message. Elijah said to Ahab, "As sure as God lives, before whom I stand, there will be neither dew nor rain these years until I say."

God knew this message would make Ahab and Jezebel angry. They would do all they could to kill Elijah. God said to Elijah, "Go away to the east. Hide yourself by the brook Cherith on this side of the Jordan River. You shall drink water from the brook, and I have commanded the ravens to feed you."

Elijah obeyed the Lord. He went to the brook Cherith to live. There he hid from King Ahab and his wicked wife Jezebel.

Every morning when it was time for breakfast, the ravens came. They brought him bread and meat to eat. Again, every evening at supper time, the ravens came. They brought him the same kind of food he had had for breakfast. Whenever Elijah became thirsty, he drank water from the brook.

All this time there was no rain and no dew in the land of Israel. At last even the brook dried up. Elijah could no longer drink from it. But Elijah did not need to worry. God had taken good care of him so far. God was still able to take good care of him.

God said to Elijah, "Get up and go to Zarephath. Zarephath was not one of the cities that belonged to the children of Israel. It belonged to Zidon, the city from which Jezebel had come. God said to Elijah, "I have commanded a widow there to feed you."

Elijah left his home by the brook Cherith. He went to the city of Zarephath. When he arrived at the gate of the city, he saw the widow. She was out gathering sticks. Elijah called to her. He said, "Please get me a little water in a jar so that I can drink."

As the widow went to get the water, Elijah called to her again. He said, "Please bring me a little piece of bread in your hand."

She answered, "As sure as God lives, I do not have bread. I have only a handful of flour in a barrel and a little oil in a bottle. See, I am gathering two sticks to prepare the food for my son and me so that we may eat it and then die." She had planned to make a fire with her two sticks. Then she would bake a little bread from the handful of flour and the little oil. She thought this would be their last meal, and they would soon die from hunger.

Elijah said to her, "Do not be afraid. Go and do as you have said. Only make a little bun first and bring it to me. After that prepare food for you and for your son. This is what the Lord said, 'The barrel of flour will not get empty. Neither shall the bottle of oil get empty until the day that the Lord sends rain on the earth.' "

The woman obeyed Elijah. She first made a bun for Elijah. Then she found enough flour and oil to make a bun for herself and her son. She and Elijah and all who lived at her house had enough to eat. The next time the widow wanted to make a meal, she still found enough flour in the barrel and oil in the bottle to make what they needed. For many days there was enough flour and oil to make still another meal. It was as the Lord had said.

One day the widow's son became so sick that

he died. His mother was afraid that her son had died because of her sin. She knew that Elijah was a man of God. She went to him to ask him about it.

Elijah said to her, "Give me your son." He carried the son upstairs to his own bedroom and laid him on his own bed. He cried to the Lord. He said, "O Lord, have You also brought evil on this woman with whom I stay by killing her son?" Then Elijah stretched himself upon the child three times. He prayed, saying, "O Lord my God, please let this child's soul come into him again."

The Lord heard the prayer of Elijah. The child's soul came into him again. He was alive! Elijah brought the child down from his bedroom and gave him back to his mother, saying, "See, your son lives!"

The woman said, "Now I know that you are a man of God and that what you say is true."

Elijah Talks to King Ahab

1 Kings 18:1–19

Three years had passed since Elijah had told Ahab that there would be no rain nor dew until he said. By this time the land was very dry. The people and the animals in Israel were suffering from lack of food and water. Ahab tried desperately to find Elijah. He had sent men to look for him in every nation and kingdom of the earth. But when God hides a man, it is wasted work to try to find him. No one can find him until God is ready.

Now God was ready to send Elijah to Ahab. God came to Elijah and said, "Go to Ahab. Tell him I will send rain on the earth." So Elijah started out to go to Ahab.

Ahab did not know that Elijah was on the way with the news that rain was coming soon. Ahab called Obadiah, a ruler of his house. He said, "Go into the land to all fountains of water and to all brooks. See if we may be able to find grass to keep our horses and mules alive so we do not lose all the animals."

Ahab and Obadiah divided the land between themselves to look for water and pasture. Ahab went one way by himself, and Obadiah went another way by himself.

Obadiah was a righteous man. He was afraid to disobey God. Before this, Ahab's wicked wife Jezebel had killed many prophets of the Lord. At that time Obadiah had taken one hundred prophets and had hid them in a cave so that Jezebel could not find them to kill them. He had fed them with bread and water to keep them alive.

Now as Obadiah was on his way to find pasture for the animals, Elijah met him. Obadiah fell down on his face. He asked, "Are you my lord Elijah?"

Elijah said, "I am. Go and tell the king I am here."

Obadiah was afraid to tell Ahab that he had seen Elijah. He was afraid God's spirit would hide Elijah again so that Ahab could not find him. Then Ahab would think that he had lied to him and would kill him. Obadiah said to Elijah, "What have I sinned that you cause Ahab to kill me? Did no one tell you that when Jezebel killed the prophets of the Lord, I hid one hundred of them in a cave and fed them with bread and water? If I tell Ahab you are here, he will kill me."

But Elijah did not mean for any harm to come to Obadiah. He said, "As the Lord lives, before whom I stand, I will surely show myself to Ahab today."

Obadiah believed Elijah and went to meet Ahab. He said to Ahab, "I have seen Elijah."

Ahab went to meet Elijah. Now Ahab thought that it was Elijah's fault that there was no rain. He thought the people and animals were suffering because Elijah had said there would be no rain. But the famine had come because of Ahab's wickedness. God had only sent Elijah to tell Ahab how it would be. Yet Ahab blamed Elijah for bringing this trouble upon Israel. He said to Elijah, "Are you the one who is troubling Israel?"

Elijah answered, "I have not troubled Israel. You and your father's house have troubled Israel by disobeying God's commands and by following Baal. Now send for all the people of Israel. Call the four hundred fifty prophets of Baal and the four hundred prophets of the groves, who eat at Jezebel's table. Gather them together to Mount Carmel."

"The Lord, He Is the God"

1 Kings 18:20–40

Ahab gathered all the children of Israel and the prophets together at Mount Carmel.

Elijah came before this great congregation of people at Mount Carmel. He said, "How long will you be in doubt between two opinions? If the Lord is God, follow Him. But if Baal is God, follow him."

The people did not answer Elijah one word.

Elijah said to the people, "I am the only one who is still a prophet of the Lord. But Baal has 450 prophets. Let them give us two bullocks. Let the prophets of Baal choose one bullock for themselves. Let them cut it into pieces and lay it on wood, but put no fire under it. You call on your gods, and I will call on the Name of the Lord. The God that answers by sending fire, let Him be God."

The people thought that this was a fair test. They said to Elijah, "What you have said is good."

Elijah said to the prophets of Baal, "Choose one bullock for yourselves. You can dress yours first because there are many of you. Call on the name of your gods, but put no fire under the bullock."

The prophets of Baal did as Elijah said. They dressed the bullock and laid it in the wood. Then they called on their god, Baal, to send fire to burn up their sacrifice. From morning till noon they kept calling, "O Baal, hear us." But Baal could not hear them. He could not answer them and send fire, for he was not the true God. He was only an idol.

The prophets of Baal were desperate to prove that Baal was God. They did all they knew to do to make Baal notice them. They jumped up and down on the altar which they had made.

How foolish this must have looked to Elijah! At noon Elijah began to made fun of them. He said, "Call loudly, for Baal is a god. Either he is talking or going after someone or is on a journey. Maybe he is sleeping and must be awakened."

The prophets called loudly. They cut themselves with knives till the blood gushed out. They kept trying to make Baal hear them until the evening. But all that they did was useless. An idol cannot see, hear, or do anything. Baal did not answer them or pay any attention to them.

The time to hold the evening sacrifice drew near. Elijah said to all the people, "Come near to me."

All the people came near to Elijah. Then Elijah repaired the altar of the Lord that was broken down. He used twelve stones to build it— one stone for each of the twelve tribes of Israel. After the altar was built, Elijah made a ditch around it. He laid wood in the proper place upon the altar. He cut up the bullock and laid it upon the wood. Then he said, "Fill four barrels with water. Pour it on the burnt sacrifice and the wood."

Four barrels were filled with water. It was poured on the burnt sacrifice and on the wood. Everything was very wet.

Elijah said, "Do it the second time."

Again, the second time, four barrels were filled with water. They were poured upon the wood and upon the burnt offering.

Elijah said, "Do it the third time."

For the third time, four barrels of water were filled. They were poured on the burnt sacrifice and on the wood. The water ran around the altar. The

ditch was also filled with water.

Now it was time for the evening sacrifice. Elijah the prophet came near to the altar. He said, "Lord God of Abraham, Isaac, and Israel, let these people know today that You are God and that I am Your servant. Let them know that I have done these things because You wanted me to do them. Hear me, O Lord, hear me, that these people may know that You are the Lord God."

Elijah was speaking to the true and living God. God heard the prayer of His servant who trusted in Him. The fire of the Lord fell. It burned up the sacrifice and the wood on which the bullock was laid. But that was not all. It also burned up the stones. It even licked up the water that was in the ditch around the altar.

All the people saw this amazing thing. They fell on their faces. They said, "The Lord, He is the God! The Lord, He is the God!"

Elijah commanded, "Catch the prophets of Baal. Do not let one of them escape."

The people caught the prophets of Baal. Elijah brought them to the brook Kishon and killed them there.

Elijah Flees From Jezebel

1 Kings 18:41–19:8

After the prophets of Baal had been killed, Elijah talked to King Ahab. He said, "Go and eat and drink, because I hear a sound. It tells me that there will be an abundance of rain."

While Ahab was going, Elijah left the brook Kishon, where the prophets of Baal had been killed. He went up again to the top of Mount Carmel. There on the top of the mountain, he threw himself on the ground. He put his face between his knees and prayed to God to send rain again on the earth.

Elijah said to his servant, "Go and look toward the sea."

The servant went to look. But he saw no clouds in the sky. There was no sign of rain. He came back to Elijah and said, "There is nothing."

Elijah said to him, "Go again."

The servant still did not see anything. Elijah told him to go and look seven times. Seven times the servant went to look for a sign of rain. He saw nothing until the seventh time. Then he saw one little cloud. He told his master, "See, there is a little cloud like a man's hand rising out of the sea."

Even though the cloud was very small, Elijah knew that his prayer was answered. He said to his servant, "Go and say to Ahab, 'Get your chariot ready and go down so that the rain does not stop you.'"

In the meantime, the sky became black with clouds. The wind blew. Rain fell thick and fast. Ahab rode in his chariot to Jezreel. But the hand of the Lord was on Elijah so that he was able to run very fast. He ran to Jezreel ahead of Ahab.

Ahab told his wife Jezebel all the things that Elijah had done. He told her that Elijah had killed all the prophets of Baal with a sword.

Jezebel was furious! She made up her mind to kill Elijah, and quickly, too! She sent a messenger to Elijah with this message: "Let the gods kill me if I do not kill you by tomorrow about this time."

Elijah would take no chances with a wicked woman like Jezebel. He fled for his life. He went to one of the cities in the land of Judah. There in that city he left his servant while he traveled on for another day into the wilderness.

In the wilderness Elijah sat down under a juniper tree. He was tired of being hunted and of having to hide. He wished that he could die. He said to the Lord, "I have had enough. Now, O Lord, take away my life; for I am no better than my fathers."

As Elijah lay there under the juniper tree, he fell asleep. After a while he was awakened. An angel had touched him. The angel said to him, "Get up and eat."

Elijah looked to see what there was to eat. he saw a cake baked on coals of fire. A bottle of water was right by his head. Elijah ate the cake and drank the water. Then he lay down again.

The angel of the Lord came to him the second time. He touched Elijah and said, "Get up and eat because the journey is too great for you."

Elijah got up and ate and drank again. This was his last meal for forty days and forty nights. But God blessed those two meals to give Elijah all the strength he needed for his journey. For forty days and forty nights Elijah traveled to Mount Horeb, the mountain of God.

There at Mount Horeb, Elijah lived in a cave to hide from Jezebel.

God Speaks to Elijah

1 Kings 19:9–21

While Elijah was hiding in the cave at Mount Horeb, God came to him. He said, "What are you doing here, Elijah?"

Elijah answered, "I have been very jealous for the Lord God of hosts. This is because the children of Israel have not kept their promise to You. They have thrown down Your altars and have killed Your prophets with the sword. I am the only prophet of God that is left, and they are looking for me to kill me."

God said to Elijah, "Go out and stand upon the mountain before the Lord."

Elijah went out of the cave. He stood on the mountain of God. Then the Lord passed by. A great, strong wind tore the mountains. It broke the rocks in pieces. But the Lord was not in the wind.

After the wind died down, there was an earthquake. The earth shook, but the Lord was not in the earthquake.

After the earthquake, there was a fire. But the Lord was not in the fire.

After the fire, there was a still, small voice. When Elijah heard the still, small voice, he wrapped his face in his mantle. The mantle was a loose cloak that he wore over his other clothes. Then Elijah went and stood at the entrance of the cave.

A voice came to him there and said, "What are you doing here, Elijah?"

Elijah answered again as he had answered before. He said, "I have been very jealous for the Lord God of hosts because the children of Israel have not kept their promise to You. They have thrown down Your altars and killed Your prophets with the sword. I am the only one left, and they are looking for me to kill me."

The Lord said to Elijah, "There are still seven thousand people in Israel who have not bowed down to Baal. Go and return on the way to the wilderness of Damascus. When you get to Damascus, anoint Hazael to be king over Syria and anoint Jehu to be king over Israel. You shall anoint Elisha to be prophet in your place. This is what will happen. Whoever escapes being killed by Hazael, Jehu will kill. And whoever escapes the sword of Jehu, Elisha will kill." God was getting ready for Hazael, Jehu, and Elisha to destroy the wicked house of Ahab.

What courage this must have given to Elijah! He had felt very much alone. He had thought that God's people had forsaken the Lord. True, many had. Yet God was now telling him that there were still seven thousand people in Israel who had not worshiped Baal. Yes, though the wicked people were many, God still had his faithful ones, and He intended to punish the wicked.

Now Elijah knew, too, that it was not yet time for him to die. God still had work for him to do. He must get another prophet ready to take his place.

Elijah left his hiding place in the cave at Mount Horeb. He went to do the work God had given him to do. He found Elisha plowing with twelve yoke of oxen in front of him. Elisha was with the twelfth yoke of oxen. Elijah passed by Elisha and threw his mantle upon him.

Elisha left his oxen and ran after Elijah. He said, "Please let me kiss my father and mother. Then I will follow you."

Elijah said, "Go back again, for what have I done to you?"

Elisha went back. He took a yoke of oxen and killed them. He boiled the meat and gave it to the people. Then Elisha went after Elijah and helped him in his work.

The Syrians Fight Against Israel

1 Kings 20:1–21

Ben-hadad, the king of Syria, prepared to fight against Samaria, the capital city of Israel. He got his people together, and horses and chariots. Besides his own people, he got thirty-two other kings to help him take over the city of Samaria.

Ben-hadad sent messengers to Ahab, king of Israel. They said, "This is what Ben-hadad says, 'Your gold and silver are mine. Your wives also and your children, even the best of them, are mine.'"

Ahab, king of Israel, did not want to start a quarrel with the king of Syria. He said, "My lord, O king, just as you have said, I and everything that I have is yours."

Again the messengers came from Ben-hadad to Ahab. They said, "This is what Ben-hadad says: 'Although I have sent word to you to give me your silver and gold and your wives and children, yet I will send my servants tomorrow about this time. They will search your house and the houses of your servants. Whatever they see that is pleasant in your eyes, they will take with them.'"

After Ahab received this message, he called for the older men of his kingdom. He said, "Please take notice how Ben-hadad is trying to do me harm."

All the older men and the people gave advice to the king. They said, "Do not listen to him or do what he says."

King Ahab did as they advised him to do. He sent Ben-hadad's messengers back to Ben-hadad with this message: "All that you asked me to do the first time, I will do. But this thing I may not do."

The messengers returned to Ben-hadad with Ahab's answer. Ben-hadad sent word back to Ahab. He boasted about the many people he had in his army in comparison to the few people of Ahab's army.

King Ahab told his servants what to answer King Ben-hadad. He said, "Tell him, 'Do not let him that puts on his harness boast as he that takes it off.' " This probably meant about the same as when we say, "Do not count your chickens before they are hatched." In other words,

"Do not boast about what you can do until you have done it."

Ben-hadad received this message from Ahab while he and the other kings with him were drinking. He told his servants, "Get ready to fight."

A prophet of God came to Ahab. He said, "This is what the Lord says: 'Have you seen this large group of people? I will deliver them over to you today. And you will know that I am the Lord.'"

Ahab asked the prophet, "Who shall go out to fight against the Syrians? Who shall be captain over them?"

The prophet answered, "The young princes shall go, and you shall be captain over them."

Ahab counted the young princes. There were two hundred thirty-two. Besides them, there were seven thousand men of Israel. They went out about noon to fight against Ben-hadad and his large army.

Now Ben-hadad and the thirty-two kings that were with him were drunk at this time. When his servants told him that men had come out of Samaria, he said, "Whether they have come to make peace or whether they have come to make war, take them alive."

When the Syrians came out to fight, Israel killed many of them. The other Syrians fled. King Ahab and his men ran after them and killed many of them. But Ben-hadad escaped on a horse with his horsemen.

Lesson 14

The Syrians Return

1 Kings 20:22–34

After Israel had killed many Syrians and they were sent back to their own land, the prophet came to King Ahab. He said, "Make yourself strong and see what you do, because the king of Syria will come up to fight with you again. He will come in a year from now."

That is exactly what happened. The servants of the king of Syria thought they knew why Israel had been able to overcome them. They thought they knew how they could win the next battle. So they came to their king and said, "Their gods are the gods of the hills. That is why they were stronger than we. Let us fight against them in the plain. Then surely we will be stronger than they. Do this thing. Take away the kings and put captains in their places. Get together as large an army as the one you lost. Get other horses and chariots to take the place of all those that were destroyed. We will fight against Israel in the plain. Then surely we will be stronger than they."

This advice sounded good to Ben-hadad, king of Syria. He got ready to fight. This time he did not call other kings to help him. He put captains in their places. He got together a large army, many horses and many chariots. Then he and his people went up again to fight against Israel.

But King Ahab had been warned by the prophet that they would come, and he was ready for them. They came a year later—right when the prophet had said they would come. Israel went out against them. Israel was a small group in comparison to the great Syrian army. They were like two little flocks of kids, but the Syrians filled the country.

A man of God came to talk to the king of Israel. He said, "This is what the Lord says: 'Because the Syrians said that the Lord is God of the hills and not of the valleys, I will deliver all the great multitude into your hand. You shall know that I am the Lord.'"

For seven days the armies of Israel and the armies of Syria were separated into two camps against each other. On the seventh day they came together. That day Israel killed one hundred thousand Syrians. The rest of the Syrians ran away into a city. There a wall fell on twenty-seven thousand of them. Again, Ben-hadad escaped being killed. He went inside the city and hid himself in a bedroom.

His servants said to him, "We have heard that the kings of Israel are merciful kings. Please let us put on sackcloth and go to the king of Israel to see if he might let you live."

The servants of Ben-hadad put on sackcloth. Then they went to King Ahab and said, "Your servant Ben-hadad says, 'Please let me live.'"

Ahab answered, "Is he still alive? He is my brother."

The servants of Ben-hadad watched very closely to see how King Ahab really felt toward them. They took special note of what he said.

King Ahab said, "Go and bring him."

Ben-hadad came to the king of Israel. He said, "I will give back to you the cities which my father took from your father. And you shall make streets for you in Damascus as my father made in Samaria."

Ahab promised to let Ben-hadad live if he would do this. This was not pleasing to God. God had been with Israel to help them kill the Syrians. He did not want them to let Ben-hadad, the king of Syria, live.

Ahab Sins More

1 Kings 20:35–21:10

A certain man of the sons of the prophets said to his neighbor, "Please hit me."

Since God wanted the prophet to say this, God wanted the neighbor to hit him. But his neighbor would not do it.

The son of the prophet said, "Because you did not do what the Lord said, as soon as you leave me, a lion will kill you."

This happened. As soon as the neighbor left, a lion found him and killed him.

The son of the prophet found another man. He said to him, "Please hit me."

This man obeyed the word of God by the prophet. He hit and wounded the son of the prophet.

Then the wounded prophet left. He waited along the way for King Ahab. He had disguised his face with ashes so that the king could not tell who he was.

As King Ahab came by, the son of the prophet

called to him. He said, "I went out into the middle of the battle. A man came over and brought a man to me. He said to me, 'Keep this man. If for any reason yo let him get away, you will have to take his place or else pay money.' As I was busy with other things, the man I was to keep got away."

King Ahab did not show pity to this man. He thought he deserved his punishment for being careless and letting the other man escape.

Then the son of the prophet hurried and took the ashes away from his face. The king saw that he was one of the prophets. Then the prophet had more to say to Ahab. He said, "This is what the Lord says, 'Because you let a man go that I wanted destroyed, your life will have to go for his life and your people for his people.'"

King Ahab understood this message. He had let Ben-hadad, king of Syria, live and go back to his own land when God wanted him destroyed. He and his people would have to die because he had done this. He did not deserve any pity either. He deserved the punishment. Ahab went home to Samaria feeling very heavy-hearted and displeased.

Next to the palace of King Ahab was a vineyard that belonged to a man named Naboth.

Ahab thought Naboth's vineyard would be a handy place for a garden. He wanted it for his own. Ahab said to Naboth, "Sell me your vineyard. I want it for a garden of herbs because it is near my house. I will give you a better vineyard for this one. Or, if you would rather, I will pay you what your vineyard is worth."

But Naboth did not want to sell his vineyard. It had belonged to his father and to his fathers before him. God wanted His people to keep the land that had been handed down to them from their fathers. Naboth knew this. He said to Ahab, "The Lord does not want me to sell you what I inherited from my fathers."

Ahab was very much displeased because Naboth refused to sell the vineyard to him. He had counted on having it for his own. He went to his house and lay down on his bed. He turned his face to the wall and pouted like a naughty child does when he cannot have his own way. He would not eat.

His wife Jezebel did not know what was wrong with him. She said, "Why are you so sad that you will not eat?"

Ahab answered, "Because I said to Naboth, 'Sell me your vineyard for money. Or, if you would rather, I will give you another vineyard for it.' But he said that he would not give it to me."

Jezebel said to Ahab, "Are you not ruling the kingdom of Israel? Get up and eat and be happy. I will give you the vineyard of Naboth."

Wicked Jezebel wrote letters and signed Ahab's name to them. She sealed them with his seal and sent them to the rulers of the city. This is what she wrote in the letters:

> Make an announcement that there is to be a fast. Set Naboth up in a high place among the people. Set two evil men before Naboth to say evil things against him. Have them say about him, "You spoke evil about God and the king." Then carry him out and stone him so that he will die.

Ahab Humbles Himself

1 Kings 21:11–29

The rulers of the city received their letters from Jezebel. They saw Ahab's name signed to them. They saw his seal. They prepared to do as Jezebel had written, thinking it was the king's orders.

The rulers announced that there should be a fast. When the people gathered together for the fast, the rulers set Naboth up in a high place. In the presence of the people, two evil men said to Naboth, "You spoke evil about God and the king." Then they carried Naboth away and stoned him with stones so that he died.

After this, word was sent to Jezebel, saying, "Naboth is stoned and is dead."

When Jezebel heard this, she went to Ahab. She said, "Get up and take possession of the vineyard of Naboth that he refused to sell to you. Naboth is dead."

When Ahab heard that Naboth was dead, he got up to go to the vineyard of Naboth. He was going to claim it for himself. But just because Naboth was dead did not make it his. God knew that Ahab had wanted what did not belong to him. This was covetousness, and God had said in His Law, "Thou shalt not covet." Also God knew that an innocent man had been killed so that Ahab could have what he wanted. God had also said in His Law, "Thou shalt not kill." God would not let such great wickedness go unpunished.

God said to Elijah, "Get up and go down to meet Ahab, king of Israel in Samaria. He is in the vineyard of Naboth. He has gone there to take possession of it for himself. Tell him that this is what I say, 'Have you killed and also taken this for your own? In the place where the dogs licked the blood of Naboth, the dogs will lick you blood, even yours.'"

Elijah went to the vineyard of Naboth and met Ahab there. When Ahab saw Elijah he said to him, "Have you found me, O my enemy?"

Elijah answered, "I have found you. Because you have sold yourself to do evil in the sight of the Lord, I will bring evil upon you and take away your children. The dogs will eat Jezebel. The dogs will eat those of your house who die in the city. The birds of the air will eat those who die in the field."

This was a severe punishment, indeed; but it was fair, as God's punishments always are. There was no one who did wickedness in God's sight like Ahab. His wife Jezebel had stirred him up to do many of his wicked deeds.

When Ahab heard what God had spoken by His prophet Elijah, he began to think seriously. He knew that he had sinned greatly. He wanted to show that he was sorry for what he had done. He tore his clothes and dressed himself in sackcloth.

God said to Elijah, "Do you see how Ahab has humbled himself? Because he has humbled himself before Me, I will not bring the evil upon him in his days. In his son's days, I will bring evil upon his house."

Craig

Jehoshaphat, a Good King of Judah

1 Kings 22:1–9; 2 Chronicles 17:1–18:8

While the ten tribes of Israel had wicked Ahab for their king, the people of Judah had a very good king. His name was Jehoshaphat. He was a son of the good king Asa. Because Jehoshaphat obeyed the Lord, the Lord was with him. Jehoshaphat did not follow the ways of the kings of Israel. The people of Judah appreciated having a good king. They brought him presents, and he became very rich.

Jehoshaphat was careful to obey God, and he wanted his people to obey God, too. To obey God, the people needed to know God's laws. So Jehoshaphat sent teachers out into the cities of Judah to teach the people the ways of the Lord. They went into all the cities of the land of Judah and taught the people from the Book of the Law of the Lord.

Because Jehoshaphat and his people knew God's laws and obeyed them, they were strong. And because they were strong, the people in the other kingdoms were afraid to come and fight against them. Instead of fighting against him, some of his enemies even brought him presents. The Philistines brought him presents of silver. The Arabians gave him seven thousand, seven hundred rams and seven thousand, seven hundred goats.

Jehoshaphat built cities in which to store his things. He also built castles. He had much business in the cities of Judah. At Jerusalem he had many mighty men to help him in his business. Altogether he had over a million helpers, besides the men whom he put in the fenced cities of Judah. These men were also prepared to fight if enemies should come out against them.

Although Jehoshaphat was a good king, he did a very unwise thing. He made an agreement to work with Ahab, the wicked king of Israel. Jehoshaphat came down to Ahab, king of Israel. To honor Jehoshaphat, king of Judah, Ahab killed many animals for him and his people.

At this time there was peace between Israel and Syria. It had now been three years since the people of Syria had come to fight against them. Now Ahab was ready to go and fight against the Syrians, and he wanted Jehoshaphat to help him.

Ahab asked Jehoshaphat, "Will you go with me to battle?"

Jehoshaphat answered, "I am as you are. My people are as your people. My horses are as your horses." By saying this, Jehoshaphat showed that he was ready to join with Israel in battle to help them to overcome their enemies and get back the city the Syrians had taken. But first Jehoshaphat wanted to know if it was the Lord's will for Israel to go to battle. He said to Ahab, "Please ask to see what God says about this."

Ahab gathered about four hundred of his prophets together. He said to them, "Shall I go against Ramoth-gilead to fight, or shall I stay?"

All the prophets answered, "Go up, because the Lord will deliver it into the hand of the king."

Even though the four hundred prophets all agreed that Israel should go, Jehoshaphat was not satisfied. He did not trust Ahab's prophets. He said, "Is there not a prophet of the Lord besides these whom we may ask?"

Ahab answered, "There is one man whom we can ask what the Lord says, but I hate him because he does not prophesy good about me, but always evil."

Jehoshaphat answered, "Do not say that."

Then Ahab called for an officer. He said to him, "Quickly bring Micaiah." Now Micaiah was a true prophet of the Lord.

Lesson 18

Micaiah's Word Comes True

1 Kings 22:9–40; 2 Chronicles 18:9–34

Ahab's officer went to call the prophet Micaiah. He said to him, "All the other prophets have given a good message to the king. Please speak as they do and say what is good."

Micaiah answered, "As sure as God lives, what the Lord says to me, that I will say."

Micaiah came in before the king. Ahab asked him, "Shall we go to battle or not?"

Micaiah knew that Ahab did not really want to know the truth, so he only pretended to tell the truth. He said, "Go and prosper, for God will give Syria to the king."

The king suspected that Micaiah was hiding the truth from him. He said to Micaiah, "How many times shall I command you to tell me nothing but what is true in the Name of the Lord?" Poor Ahab! He was like the wicked are— never satisfied. He did not like if Micaiah hid the truth from him. But he did not like it, either, if Micaiah told him the truth, because the truth was

195

always against him. God could not speak good for Ahab because Ahab was wicked.

But now Micaiah would tell Ahab the truth. He said, "I saw all Israel scattered upon the hills as sheep that have no shepherd. The Lord said, 'These have no master. Let everyone go to his house in peace.'"

Ahab knew this meant that he would be killed. Then Israel would be without a king. Ahab said to Jehoshaphat, "Did I not tell you he would not prophesy good about me, but evil?"

Micaiah had more to say. He could tell Ahab and Jehoshaphat why the four hundred prophets had said that Ahab should go to battle and the Lord would help him. The prophets had spoken by a lying spirit. The Lord was going to destroy King Ahab in the battle.

One of the prophets whose name was Zedekiah did not like what Micaiah said. He went up to Micaiah and hit him on the cheek. He said to him, "Which way did God's Spirit go from me to talk to you?"

Micaiah answered, "You will see on that day when you go into a bedroom to hide yourself."

Ahab said to his servants, "Take Micaiah back to the ruler of the city and to Joash the king's son. Tell them to put this fellow in prison and to feed him with bread and water until I come in peace."

Micaiah said, "If you come back at all in peace, the Lord has not spoken by me. Listen, O people, every one of you."

But as Micaiah said, Ahab was persuaded by the lying spirit in the mouths of the four hundred prophets. He thought he could go to battle and prosper as they said. He and Jehoshaphat both went out to battle against the Syrians.

Ahab said to Jehoshaphat, "I will put on other clothes so the Syrians cannot tell I am the king of Israel. But you dress in your own clothes." So Ahab put on other clothes and went out to battle.

The king of Syria had thirty-two captains ready to go out to battle. He said to them, "Fight only with the king of Israel." He did not care if any other of the Israelites were killed. He did want to make sure that Ahab was killed.

So when the captains went to battle, they were all watching for Ahab. When they saw Jehoshaphat in his robes, they said, "Surely this is the king of Israel." So they closed in around him to fight with him.

Jehoshaphat saw that he was in great danger.

He cried out, and the Lord was merciful to him and helped him. God caused the Syrian captains to know that he was not the king of Israel and to let him alone. They turned away from him and did not go after him any more.

In the Syrian army there was a man who drew his bow and shot an arrow. He did not know where he was shooting. But God knew. God guided the aim so that the arrow hit Ahab. Ahab had armor on, but God guided the arrow so that it went right between the joints of the armor and wounded him. King Ahab said to the man who drove his chariot, "Take me away from the armies, for I am wounded."

The battle went on, and the people fought harder. In the evening, about the time the sun set, Ahab died. Blood ran out of Ahab's wound into the chariot. Word went out that everyone should return home. Israel had to return home without a king. They were as sheep without a shepherd.

The king of Israel was carried back to Samaria and buried there. The chariot in which he had died was washed in the pool of Samaria. There dogs licked up Ahab's blood as the Lord had said.

Ahab's son Ahaziah became king in his place.

Jehoshaphat Helps His People

1 Kings 22:41–53; 2 Chronicles 19; 20

After the battle with the Syrians, Jehoshaphat, king of Judah, returned to his house at Jerusalem.

Jehu, a prophet, went out to meet him. He said to Jehoshaphat, "Should you help the ungodly and love those who hate the Lord? The Lord is angry with you for this. Yet there is good found in you because you have taken away the groves out of the land. And you have prepared yourself to find out what God would have you to do."

Jehoshaphat lived at Jerusalem, but he was interested in all of his people wherever they lived. He went out to them to help them to come back to God and obey Him. He worked hard to see that his kingdom was ruled well. He set judges over the land to rule the people fairly. He told the judges, "Be careful what you do, because you are not judging for man but for the Lord. The Lord is not unjust. He judges fairly. If a man does wrong, He will punish him, no matter who he is. Even if he is a rich man and offers money to be free, God still punishes him." This was a good reminder to the judges. To judge right as God judges, they needed to punish those who needed punishment no matter who they were. They were not to agree with a guilty person to let him go without punishment even if he offered them money or gifts to do it. On the other hand, they were not to punish those who did not need punishment.

When the judges returned to Jerusalem after ruling in other cities of Judah, Jehoshaphat made some of them rulers in Jerusalem. He commanded them, "Do as I told you to do. Do it in the fear of God, faithfully, and with a perfect heart."

After this someone came to Jehoshaphat with startling news. He said, "A great multitude is coming against you from beyond the sea on this side of Syria."

Jehoshaphat feared when he heard this. He wanted to know what God would have him do. He asked all the people in his kingdom to fast.

From every city of Judah, people came together to fast and to pray to the Lord for help. Jehoshaphat stood in the temple with this large congregation of people. He prayed and said, "O Lord God of our fathers, are You not God in heaven? Do You not rule over all the kingdoms of the heathen? Do You not have power and might, so that no one is able to fight against You and overcome You? Are You not our God who drove out the people of this land before Your people Israel? And did You not give this land to the children of Abraham, Your friend forever? Now behold, the children of Ammon and Moab and Mount Seir. When Israel came out of the land of Egypt, You would not let Your people go into their lands. Israel turned from them and did not destroy them. Behold, I say, how they reward us evil for the good we did to them. They have come to drive us out of Your land that You gave to us. O our God, will You not judge them? We do not have any strength against this great company that is coming against us. Neither do we know what to do. But we are looking to You for help."

When Jehoshaphat had finished praying, one of the Levites stood up in the middle of the congregation. He said, "Do not be afraid because of this great multitude, because the battle is not yours, but God's. Go down against them tomorrow, for the Lord will be with you."

When Jehoshaphat and the people heard these encouraging words, they bowed and worshiped the Lord. God had already answered their prayer to show them what to do. Then the Levites and others with them stood up to praise the Lord with a loud voice.

Early the next morning, the people got out of bed and departed for the wilderness of Tekoa. As they went Jehoshaphat stood before them to encourage them. He said, "Believe in the Lord your God, and you shall be established. Believe God's prophets, and all will be well for you."

After Jehoshaphat talked some things over with the people, he chose singers to go before the army. The singers were to praise the beauty of God's holiness. They were to say, "Praise the Lord, for His mercy endures forever."

When the singers began to sing and to praise the Lord, the Lord began to work for the people of Judah. They looked at their enemies. All of them had fallen to the earth and were dead. Not one escaped.

Jehoshaphat and his people went out to take from the dead people anything that might be valuable. They found so many riches and precious jewels that it took them three days to gather them all. King Jehoshaphat led the people back to Jerusalem. They came back with music and great joy.

The people in the other kingdoms of the world heard that the Lord had fought for Judah against their enemies. They were afraid to fight against Judah for fear the Lord would also fight against them. So the kingdom of Jehoshaphat enjoyed peace and quietness.

After this, Jehoshaphat again did a very unwise thing. He joined himself to Ahaziah, the son of Ahab, king of Israel. Ahaziah was also a wicked king as his father had been. Jehoshaphat helped him to make ships to go to Tarshish. Even though Jehoshaphat had been a good king, God had to punish him for this. He broke the ships so that they could not go to Tarshish.

Later Ahaziah asked Jehoshaphat to let their servants work together. But Jehoshaphat would not do it. It seems that he had learned his lesson not to join in helping the ungodly.

"Is There No God in Israel?"

2 Kings 1

Ahaziah, king of Israel, had an accident. He fell through the lattice of an upstairs window. He became so sick that he wondered if he would ever be well again. So he sent messengers to ask an idol, a god of the heathen, whether he would get well.

God knew what Ahaziah did. He sent an angel to Elijah, saying, "Get up, and go meet the messengers of the king. Ask them why they go to ask an idol. Is there no God in Israel? Tell them that the king will not get well. He will die."

Elijah obeyed the Lord. He went to meet the messengers and tell them what God said. Elijah said to them, "Turn around, and go back to the king. Tell him this is what the Lord says: 'Why are you sending messengers to ask an idol? Is it because you do not believe there is a God in Israel? Because you did this, you shall surely die!'"

The messengers turned and went back to the

king. "Why did you come back so soon?" King Ahaziah wondered.

The messengers answered, "A man met us and said, 'Go back to the king and tell him this is what the Lord says: "Is there not a God in Israel that you send to ask an idol, one of the gods of the heathen?" ' "

King Ahaziah asked, "What kind of man was he who came to you and told you these things?"

When the messengers described the man, the king knew who it was. He said, "It is Elijah."

King Ahaziah sent a captain with fifty men to Elijah. They found him sitting on the top of a hill. The captain said to Elijah, "Man of God, the king has said, 'Come down.' "

Elijah answered, "If I am a man of God, let fire come down from heaven and destroy you and your men." God sent fire down from heaven and burned up the captain and his fifty men.

The king sent another captain with fifty men to Elijah. This captain said, "O man of God, the king has said, 'Come down quickly!' "

Again Elijah answered, "If I am a man of God, let fire come down from heaven and destroy you and your men." Again God sent fire down from heaven and burned up the captain and his fifty men.

The third time, King Ahaziah sent a captain and fifty men to Elijah. This third captain was afraid. He knew what had happened to the other groups of men. He came to the hill where Elijah was and bowed down on his knees before him. He begged Elijah and said, "O man of God, please let my life and the life of these fifty men be precious in your sight."

Then the angel of the Lord spoke to Elijah and said, "Go down with him. Do not be afraid." So Elijah arose and went back with them to the king.

He said to the king, "You sent to ask an idol, a heathen god, if you would get well. Why did you do this? Is there no God in Israel? Because you did this, you shall surely die."

Soon after this, King Ahaziah died; and Jehoram was made king in his place.

Elijah Is Taken to Heaven

2 Kings 2:1–18

The prophet Elijah had served the Lord for many years. He had worked hard to destroy idol worship in Israel. He taught the people about the true God. Now his work was nearly finished, and God wanted to take him to heaven.

God had already chosen Elisha to be the next prophet. Elisha knew that God would soon take Elijah away. The two prophets went to Gilgal. There Elijah said, "You stay here. The Lord wants me to go to Bethel."

But Elisha answered, "I will not leave you." So they went on to Bethel together.

The sons of the prophets at Bethel asked Elisha, "Do you know that Elijah will soon be taken away from you?"

Elisha answered, "Yes, I know it."

Then Elijah said to Elisha, "You stay here. The Lord wants me to go to Jericho."

"I will not leave you," Elisha answered. So they both went to Jericho.

At Jericho the sons of the prophets asked Elisha, "Do you know that Elijah will be taken away from you today?"

"Yes, I know it," answered Elisha.

Again Elijah said, "Please stay here. The Lord has sent me on to Jordan."

"I will not leave you," Elisha insisted. So the two went on together. Fifty sons of the prophets followed. They stood a long way off and watched.

Elijah and Elisha stood by the Jordan River. Elijah took off his mantle, folded it, and hit the water with it. When he did this, God caused the water to part, and they walked across on dry ground.

As they walked along on the other side Elijah asked, "What can I do for you before I am taken away?"

Elisha answered, "Please let a double portion of your spirit be upon me."

Elijah knew that only God could give this gift. He said, "You have asked a hard thing. But if you see me when I leave, you will have your request. If you do not see me leave, you will not receive it."

Elisha was very careful to stay near Elijah.

On and on they walked, talking as they went. Suddenly they saw a chariot and horses of fire coming toward them! It passed between them.

At this time Elijah was caught up in a whirlwind. It carried him up to heaven. Elisha saw his dear, old friend go up. He cried, "My father, my father! The chariot of Israel and the horsemen thereof!" Then he saw Elijah no more.

Elisha must have felt very lonely without Elijah. He took hold of his own clothes and tore them in two pieces. He looked and saw Elijah's mantle that had fallen from him as he went up in the whirlwind. Elisha picked up the mantle and walked back to the Jordan River alone. He stood on the bank, looking down into the water. Then he took Elijah's mantle, just as Elijah had done, and hit the water. He said, "Where is the God of Elijah?"

Again God parted the water and made a dry path for Elisha to cross over.

Fifty sons of the prophets were on the other side of Jordan. They said, "The spirit of Elijah is on Elisha." How happy Elisha was! God had given him his request.

The sons of the prophets bowed themselves before Elisha. "Please let us go and look for Elijah," they begged. "Maybe the Lord threw him down on some mountain or in some valley."

Elisha said, "No, you shall not go." He knew God had taken Elijah to heaven. But they kept urging him until Elisha was ashamed. Finally he said, "Go."

The men went. For three days they looked and looked. But, of course, they could not find him.

When they came back Elisha said, "Did not I tell you. 'Do not go'?"

Elisha, the Prophet of the Lord

2 Kings 2:19–3:25

Elisha stayed in Jericho for a while. The men of the city came to him and said, "This city is at a pleasant place, as you can see. But the water is not good to drink, and the land does not grow good crops."

Elisha replied, "Bring me a new bottle and put salt in it." When they brought it to Elisha, he took it to the spring where the people got their drinking water. He threw the salt into the water and said, "The Lord says, 'I have made the water pure and good. From now on no one will get sick from drinking it, and it will not hurt the land any more. The land will bear good crops.'"

After that the water was always good.

Elisha left Jericho and started back to Bethel. As he was going, some children came out of the city and followed him. They must have heard about how Elijah was taken up to heaven, because they made fun of Elisha, saying, "Go up, thou bald head. Go up, thou bald head."

God was not pleased that they were making fun of Elisha. He sent two bears out of the woods, and they hurt forty-two children.

Elisha went on to Samaria, where Jehoram, the king of Israel, lived. At this time Jehoram was having trouble. The king of Moab was coming to fight against Israel.

Jehoram asked Jehoshaphat, the king of Judah, "Will you go with me to fight against Moab?"

Jehoshaphat said, "I will go. Which way shall we go?"

Jehoram answered, "We will go through the Wilderness of Edom." So the kings of Israel, Judah, and Edom, with their servants and their animals, started out on the long, seven-day journey through the wilderness. Soon their water was all gone, and there was no water in the wilderness.

"Is there no prophet of the Lord in Israel?" asked Jehoshaphat. "We could ask him what to do."

One of the king's servants answered, "Elisha is here. The word of the Lord is with him." So they went to find Elisha.

When Elisha saw them, he said to the king of

Israel, "What do I have to do with you? Why don't you go to the prophets of your gods, the idols? If it would not be for Jehoshaphat with you, I would not even look at you." Elisha said this because Jehoram was a wicked king and worshiped idols.

Because of good King Jehoshaphat, Elisha told them that the Lord said, "Make this valley full of ditches. It shall not rain, yet there shall be enough water for you and all your animals. This is a small thing for the Lord to do. He also will deliver the Moabites into your hand."

The next morning, at the time of the offering, there was plenty of water in the land.

The people of Moab heard that the kings were coming to fight against them. They gathered together all the men who were able to fight. Early the next morning, when they got up, the sun was shining on the water that had filled the ditches. It made the water look as red as blood. The Moabites said, "This is blood. The kings are dead. The Israelites have killed each other. Let us go up and get their things."

But the Israelites were not dead. When the people of Moab got to the camp of Israel, the Israelites chased them back to their own country.

They killed many of the people along the way and destroyed many of their cities.

A Widow and a Pot of Oil

2 Kings 4:1–7

In the land of Israel there lived a poor widow who had two sons. She had been the wife of one of the young prophets who loved and served the true God. Since her husband died, she was not able to earn enough money to make a living for her family.

This poor widow came to Elisha for help. She cried, "Your servant, my husband, is dead. You know that he feared the Lord. Now I am in trouble. A man whom I owe some money came to my door to get the money. I did not have the money, so I could not pay him. He said he will come back soon, and if I do not pay the debt, he will take my two sons to be his slaves."

Elisha wanted to help the poor widow. He asked her, "What do you have in your house?"

She answered, "I do not have anything except a pot of oil."

Elisha knew God could help her. "Go home," he told her, "and borrow very many jars and pots and bowls from all your neighbors. Do not borrow only a few. Take these empty vessels to your house. After you have closed the door, pour oil from your pot into all the vessels you have borrowed."

The widow obeyed Elisha. After they had borrowed many vessels, they went into the house and shut the door. The boys must have wondered what their mother would do with all these empty jars and pots and bowls.

The boys brought the vessels to their mother. She poured oil from her pot into one of the borrowed vessels. Yet her pot did not get empty. How surprised they must have been. She filled another one, and another, and another; and still her pot was full.

At last she said, "Bring me another vessel."

Her son said, "There is not another empty vessel left in the house. All the jars and pots and bowls are full!"

Quickly she went back to Elisha. He said, "Go, sell the oil, and pay your debt. Then you and your sons can live on the money that is left over."

How thankful the poor widow was! God had helped her in time of need.

She and her sons were very happy. Now they

would not need to be separated, because they could pay the money which they owed.

> "What nation is there so great, who hath God so nigh unto them, as the Lord our God is in all things that we call upon him for?" (Deuteronomy 4:7).

A Special Room
and a Special Reward

2 Kings 4:8–37

Elisha went from one place to another, teaching the people to love and serve the true God. One day he went to the little city of Shunem. A kind woman and her husband lived there. They were very rich, but they had no children.

This woman invited Elisha to stop and eat with them. So after that, whenever he passed by that way, he always stopped at their house.

One day the kind Shunammite woman said to her husband, "I believe that this man who often comes to our house is a holy man of God. Please, let us build a little room for him. Then whenever he comes, he can go into his own little room to rest.

When the room was finished, they put in it a bed, a table, a stool, and a candlestick. The special room was ready for the special guest.

How surprised Elisha was when he came back

that way again!

Elisha said to his servant, Gehazi, "Call the kind Shunammite woman and tell her to come here."

She came up to Elisha's room.

Elisha said to Gehazi, "Tell her that she has been very kind in caring for us, and ask her what she would like to have done for her. See whether she would like to have us speak to the king for her."

"No," she answered, "I am happy and satisfied with what I have." She was content to live among her people.

When the woman left, Elisha asked, "Then what can be done for her?"

Gehazi replied, "She has no children."

"Go call her," said Elisha.

When she stood in his door again, Elisha said, "You will have a son."

"No, my lord," she answered. "You are a man of God. Do not lie to me." She was so surprised she could hardly believe it.

But she did have a son, just as Elisha had said. How happy she must have been! God had rewarded her for her kindness to His prophet. This was a very special reward!

The little boy grew. One day he went along with his father to the field. He watched the reapers cut the grain. After a while he said to his father, "My head, my head."

His father told one of the servants to carry him home to his mother. The servant carried him to his mother, and she held him on her lap until noon. Then the little boy died.

His mother was very sad. She carried him up to Elisha's room. She laid him on the bed and shut the door. Then she called to her husband and said, "Please send me a young man and a donkey so that I can go to the man of God and come back again."

Her husband wondered, "Why do you want to go to him today?" He was satisfied when she explained that she had a good purpose in going and all would be well if she went.

Then she saddled the donkey and told her servant, "Drive, go forward, and do not slow up because of me, unless I tell you."

Elisha looked up and saw her coming a long way off. He said to his servant, "Run to meet her, and ask her if all is well."

She answered, "It is well," because she did not want to tell anyone her trouble until she could tell

Elisha. She believed the man of God could help her and all would be well. When she reached Elisha, she fell at his feet, and he could see she was troubled and very sad.

When Elisha understood there was something wrong with the child, he said to Gehazi, "Hurry, take my staff and go. Do not stop to talk to anyone along the way until you lay my staff on the child's face."

But the woman did not want to return home until Elisha went along back with her, so he went along.

Elisha went up to his room, where the little boy was lying on his bed. The child lay cold and still.

First Elisha prayed to God because he knew God could do anything! Then he put his face on the child's face and his hands on the child's hands. The child's body became warm again. The child sneezed seven times. Then he opened his eyes! Elisha sent Gehazi to call the kind Shunammite woman.

When she came to Elisha's room, her son was alive! How happy she was! All was well. She deeply appreciated what was done for her.

Israel's Great God

2 Kings 4:38–44; 6:1–7

There is a God in Israel. Do you remember that Elijah asked King Ahaziah, "Is there no God in Israel?" God showed His great and marvelous power many times in Israel.

After Elisha raised the son of the Shunammite woman to life again, he went to visit the young prophets at Gilgal. There was a famine in that country.

Elisha said to his servant, "Set on a big pot and boil some soup for the sons of the prophets." One man went out in the field and gathered his lap full of wild gourds and shredded them into the soup.

As the people were eating the soup, they realized that by mistake he had gotten something poisonous in it. Someone cried out, "O man of God, there is death in the pot." The people could not eat anymore of the soup.

But Elisha was not alarmed. He requested, "Bring some meal." When they brought it, Elisha threw the meal into the pot of soup.

"Now," he said, "pour out soup for the people to eat."

When they tasted the soup, it was good. It was not harmful any more.

A man from another city near Gilgal came to visit Elisha. He brought a gift of twenty loaves of barley bread and some fresh corn in the husks. Elisha knew how much the hungry people would enjoy the bread and corn. He said to his servant, "Give this to the people to eat."

The surprised servant replied, "What! Should I set this before a hundred men? There is not nearly enough for everyone."

Again Elisha said, "Give to the people because the Lord said there will be enough and some left over." So the servant obeyed, and everyone had all he wanted to eat, and still there was some left over just as the Lord had said.

Later one of the prophets told Elisha, "This place is too small for us. Let us move down beside the Jordan and build a new house."

Elisha answered, "Go."

"Please go along with us," urged the prophets.

Elisha agreed, so they went together. When they came to Jordan, they cut down trees to build their house. As one man was working, the ax head flew off and sank into the water.

"Alas, master!" he cried, "It was a borrowed ax."

He was very much distressed because he did not know how he could ever return it.

Elisha asked, "Where did it fall?"

After the man showed him the place, Elisha cut a stick and threw it into the water.

As the astonished men stood watching, the ax head rose from the bottom of the river and floated on the water.

"Get it," Elisha told the man, so he reached out his hand and took it from the water.

Many people marveled at the mighty power of God shown by Elisha.

A Faithful Little Slave Girl

2 Kings 5:1–15

North of Israel was the country of Syria. The Syrians had never learned about the true God in heaven. They worshiped idols.

The king of Syria had a captain over his army whose name was Naaman. He was a brave and mighty man, and the king looked up to him as an honorable man. But Naaman had a terrible disease called leprosy.

During the time that Elisha was a prophet in Israel, the Syrians came to fight against the Israelites. They destroyed their cities and even took some of the people captive to be slaves.

In one city the Syrians captured a little Israelite girl and took her along back to Syria.

Naaman, the captain, took this little girl along home with him to help his wife. Even thought the little girl was far away from home and often felt sad and lonely, she did her duty faithfully. Soon she began to love her new master.

One day the little captive maid said to her

mistress, "I wish my master could go to the prophet who lives in Samaria. He could heal his leprosy!"

Someone told Naaman what the little maid had said. Even the king heard about it, and he wanted Naaman to go and see whether he really could be healed.

The king of Syria promised to send a letter to the king of Israel at Samaria to let him know that he had sent Naaman. Since the king of Syria did not know the true God, he thought the king of Samaria was the great and powerful one. This is what the letter said:

> I am sending my servant Naaman to you with this letter that you may cure him of his leprosy.

When the king of Israel read the letter, he was so troubled that he tore his clothes. He was a wicked man and did not have the power of God to heal leprosy. He thought the king of Syria had asked him to do something impossible just so he could start a quarrel against him.

When Elisha heard that the king was so distressed, he went to him and asked, "Why did you tear your clothes? Send the man to me, and he shall know that there is a prophet in Israel."

So Naaman went with his horses and chariot and stood at Elisha's door. Elisha sent out a messenger to tell him, "Go and wash seven times in the Jordan River, and you will be made well."

This was not at all what Naaman expected, and he became very angry. He said to his servants, "I thought he would surely come out himself, and call on the name of the Lord his God, and put his hand over the place and heal me. Are not the rivers in Syria better than all the waters of Israel? Can I not wash in them and be clean?" Naaman turned away in anger to leave.

His servants came to him and said, "My father, if the prophet would have told you to do some great thing, would you not have done it? This is such a simple thing. Why do you not do what he said?" they urged.

So Naaman went down and dipped himself in the muddy water of the Jordan River. He looked at himself. Still the spots of leprosy were there. Again and again he dipped—three, four, five, six times—but nothing happened. The seventh time he dipped into the muddy water the spots disappeared. The leprosy was cured, just as the man of God had said! Naaman obeyed, and God healed him.

"Now I know," cried Naaman joyfully, "that there is a God in Israel!"

Lesson 27

"Be Sure Your Sin
Will Find You Out"

2 Kings 5:15–27

Naaman was thankful for what was done for him. He and all his servants went back to Elisha. Naaman said, "Now I know that there is no God in all the earth but in Israel." He offered money and rich gifts to Elisha for healing him of his leprosy. But Elisha refused to take gifts for what the Lord had done.

Naaman told Elisha that he wanted to worship the true God. He wanted the Lord to pardon him for offering sacrifices to idols. He promised that from now on he would not offer any offering to other gods, but to the true God only.

Elisha said, "Go in peace." So Naaman and his servants started out on their homeward journey.

Gehazi, Elisha's servant, saw the rich gifts that Naaman had offered to give. He allowed covetous thoughts in his heart. He wanted some of those riches for himself. Gehazi said to himself, "My master did not take any of the things that Naaman offered him, but I will run after him and take something."

Naaman had not gone far when he looked back and saw Gehazi coming. When he saw him, he got down from his chariot to meet him. "Is everything all right?" he called.

"All is well," Gehazi answered. "My master sent me to tell you that two young prophets have come to him. Please give them some money and two sets of clothes."

Gladly Naaman sent these things to Elisha. He believed Gehazi and sent twice the amount of money that Gehazi asked for. He even loaded the gifts on his own servants to carry them back for Gehazi. When they came to the tower, Gehazi took the things and hid them and let the men go on their way again.

Gehazi did not want anyone to know what he had done. First he coveted; then he lied to Naaman. Now he thought no one knew about it.

After the men departed, Gehazi went in to wait on his master. Elisha asked, "Where have you been, Gehazi?"

Gehazi answered, "Your servant has not been

anywhere."

But Elisha knew where Gehazi had been. He knew when Naaman got down from his chariot to meet Gehazi. He knew Gehazi had lied to Naaman. And now he lied again to cover up his sin.

Elisha said to Gehazi, "Because you wanted riches more than you wanted to please God, Naaman's leprosy will be on you and your children forever.

Gehazi looked at his skin, and it was white with leprosy. Now Gehazi realized that sin cannot be hidden.

God Protects His People

2 Kings 6:8–23

Ben-hadad, king of Syria, went out to fight against Israel. He told his servants his plans for the battle. Of course, he did not want the Israelites to know. If the Syrians could keep their plans secret, they would have a better chance to take the camp of Israel by surprise.

Several times the Syrians went to attack a city in Israel. But each time, to their surprise, King Jehoram had the city guarded. Ben-hadad and his soldiers tried to take other cities. Every time, the Israelites were ready for them and drove them back. Ben-hadad could not understand how the king of Israel always knew which city he was going to attack and was prepared to defeat him.

The king of Syria was very troubled about this. He thought that one of his servants must be telling King Jehoram his plans. He called his servants together. "Which of you is telling King Jehoram our secret plans?" he asked.

One of them answered, "None of us, O King.

But Elisha, the prophet in Israel, tells the king the words you say in your bedroom. He warns the king which city you plan to attack next. Then the king sends his soldiers to protect that city."

The king of Syria commanded his men, "Go and find out where Elisha is. Then I will capture him."

Someone told the king that Elisha was at Dothan. Quickly Ben-hadad sent horses and chariots and many soldiers to Dothan. That night they surrounded the city where Elisha was staying.

Early the next morning Elisha's servant looked out. He saw the horses and chariots and the great multitude of people surrounding the city. In fear he cried out, "Oh, Master, what shall we do? The Syrians are coming in from every direction."

"Do not be afraid," Elisha answered calmly. "There are more with us than with the Syrians." Then he prayed, "Lord, open the eyes of my servant that he may see."

The Lord opened his eyes, and he could see things that people cannot usually see. How surprised he must have been! When he looked, he saw the mountain was full of the Lord's horses and chariots of fire. God had sent them to protect Elisha. Now he was not afraid. He knew the Lord was caring for them.

As the Syrians came nearer, Elisha prayed, "Lord, please make these people blind."

The Lord made all the Syrians blind, as Elisha had requested. Then Elisha met them and said, "Follow me, and I will lead you to the man for whom you are looking." They could not see, so they did not know they were talking with Elisha.

Elisha led the Syrians right into the city of Samaria, where King Jehoram lived. Again Elisha prayed, "Lord, open the eyes of these people so they can see." When the Lord took away their blindness, they saw they were in the middle of the city of Samaria.

When the king of Israel saw them, he said to Elisha, "My father, shall I kill them?"

"No," answered Elisha, "you shall not hurt them. Would you kill the people whom you have taken captive? Give them food that they may eat and drink and return to their homes."

The king prepared a big meal for them. When they finished eating and drinking, he sent them away. The Syrians had come to capture Elisha, but they had no power to hurt him. Elisha had a great God who took care of him.

After this time the Syrians never again tried to capture Elisha.

Lesson 29

A Terrible Famine

2 Kings 6:24–7:2

The people in Israel were in great trouble. Ben-hadad, king of Syria, had gathered his army together again. He went up to take possession of Samaria. Day after day the Syrians waited for the Israelites to open the gate. But the Israelites did not open it.

The king of Syria knew that the Israelites would starve if he waited long enough. All their fields were outside the city. There was no way for the people to get their food. They became more and more hungry. The rich people paid high prices for only a very small amount of food. But soon the food was all gone.

The people became so hungry that they ate things which are not fit to eat because they were so desperate for food.

One day when the king was out walking on the wall, a woman cried to him for help. He said, "If the Lord does not help you, how can I help you? What do you want?"

She answered, "This woman said to me, 'Give your son that we may eat him today, and we will eat my son tomorrow.' So we boiled my son and ate him. But the next day when I said to her, 'Give your son,' she had hidden her son."

When the king heard these terrible things, he tore his clothes. Then the people saw that he was wearing sackcloth. He had put it on under his other clothes. That showed how sad he was about the great trouble in Samaria.

The king blamed Elisha for this trouble. He was very angry with Elisha and determined to kill him. Perhaps it was because Elisha had not let him kill the Syrians but had told him to feed them instead. The king sent a man to get Elisha.

Elisha was sitting in his house with some older men. Before the messenger got there, Elisha knew he was coming. He also knew that the king was planning to have him killed. He told the older men, "When the messenger comes, shut the door and hold him fast until the king arrives."

When they came, Elisha boldly told the king, "Tomorrow about this time of the day, good food will be sold very cheaply in the gates of Samaria."

This was welcome news to the starving people, but it seemed almost too good to be true.

A ruler who was with the king exclaimed, "Even if the Lord would make windows in heaven, could this be possible?"

Elisha replied, "You will see it with your eyes, but because you did not believe, you will not be able to eat any of it."

Plenty in Israel

2 Kings 7:3–20

Four men with leprosy sat at the gate of the city of Samaria. Because they had this terrible disease, they could not live among the other people.

"Why do we sit here until we die?" they said to one another. If we go into the city, there is a famine and we will die. If we just sit here, we will die also. Let us go to the camp of the Syrians. Maybe they will save us alive. And if they kill us, we will just die." Because they felt they had nothing to lose, the four lepers decided to go to the enemy camp to see if they might give them some food.

At twilight that evening the Lord had caused the Syrians to hear a noise. It sounded like horses and chariots and a great multitude of people. The Syrians were very much afraid. They thought the Israelites had hired kings of other nations to fight against them. Quickly they fled from their camp, leaving their tents and food and animals behind.

As they ran, they dropped some of their treasures.

And so it was that the four lepers found the Syrian camp with plenty of food but with no people in it. The lepers went from one tent to another. They ate and drank until they were satisfied. They carried out silver and gold and clothes and hid them.

Then one of the lepers said to the others. "This is a day of good news!" Back inside the walls of Samaria the suffering people did not know what was going on in the Syrian camp that night. The lepers thought about the starving people in the city. They did not want to be selfish, so they decided to go quickly and tell the good news to the king.

They returned to the city and called to the porter at the gate, "We came to the camp of the Syrians, and there was no one there! Horses and donkeys were tied outside, and the tents were left just as they had been."

The porters spread the good news. Even King Jehoram was awakened to hear the message of the lepers. It was still night, but King Jehoram got up and called his servants. He thought the Syrians were trying to trick them into opening their gates. He said, "They know we are hungry, so they went out and hid themselves in the field. They said that when we come out of the city, they will capture us and come and take our city."

One of the king's servants persuaded the king to let a few go and see. Finally he gave them permission.

Soon they returned with the news that they could find none of the Syrians. "But all along the way, we found clothes and dishes which the Syrians dropped in their hurry to get away." By this they knew the Syrians had been frightened, and left in great haste. They were not hiding, as the king had thought.

The Israelites crowded out the city gate to go to the Syrian camp and gather the things which were left in the tents. There was plenty of food and to spare.

King Jehoram appointed one of his rulers to be in charge of the gate. It was the same ruler who had been with Jehoram when Elisha told him, "Tomorrow this time there will be plenty of food," and he had not believed him. You remember Elisha had told him that because he did not believe it, he would see the food, but he would not eat any of it.

Now food was being sold very cheaply at the

gate. The people crowded and pushed as they rushed through the gate. This ruler was knocked down and trampled to death. He had seen the food, but he did not get to eat it, just as Elisha had said.

Unit Three

Stories of the Last Kings and Prophets

The King of Israel Meets the Shunammite Woman

2 Kings 8

God showed Elisha that there would be a famine in the land of Israel. It would last for seven years.

Elisha told the Shunammite woman with whom he stayed, "There will be a famine in the land. Arise, you and your family, and go live wherever you can. The Lord has shown me that the famine will last seven years."

The woman and her family moved to the land of the Philistines. They lived there for seven years. Then at the end of seven years, they decided to return to their home.

But when they got back to the land of Israel, they found that someone else had taken their house and land. They did not know what to do. So the woman decided to go to the king for help. She would ask him to give back her house and land. As she and her son walked along, they did not know what was happening at the king's house right at that time.

The king was talking with Gehazi, Elisha's servant, about Elisha. "Tell me more," the king said. "Please tell me all the great things that Elisha has done."

Gehazi was telling the king that Elisha had raised a woman's son to life. While he was still talking, the Shunammite woman came in to ask the king for her house and land.

Gehazi said, "O King, this is the woman; and this is her son, whom Elisha brought back to life."

The king asked the woman about it, and she told him that it was true. So the king appointed one of his officers to help the woman. He commanded, "Give her back her house and land. Give her everything that was hers. Give her back all the crops that were raised on her land from the time she left until now."

After this Elisha went to Damascus, where Ben-hadad, the king of Syria, lived. Ben-hadad was sick at this time. Someone told him that Elisha, the man of God, had come. So he called for his servant, Hazael. He said, "Take a gift and go to meet the man of God. Ask him if I will recover from my sickness."

Hazael did as he was told to do. He took a very large gift. It as so large that it took forty camels to carry it all. When Hazael stood before Elisha, he said, "Ben-hadad, king of Syria, wants to know if he will recover of his sickness."

Elisha said, "Tell him that he certainly may recover. But the Lord has shown me that he will surely die." Then Elisha began to weep.

"Why are you weeping?" asked Hazael.

Elisha answered, "Because the Lord has shown me that you will be king of Syria, and I know the evil things that you will do to the children of Israel. You will kill and destroy."

Hazael could hardly believe the terrible things that he would do. He said, "Am I a dog, that I should do these things?"

Then Hazael went back to the king. The king asked, "What did Elisha say?"

Hazael said, "He told me you would get well."

The next day Hazael took a thick cloth and dipped it in water and covered King Ben-hadad's face so that he could not breathe. After he died, Hazael became king in his place.

At this time Joram was king in Israel. He was the son of wicked King Ahab, and he followed the evil ways of his father.

Jehoram, king of Judah, had married wicked Athaliah, the daughter of Ahab and Jezebel. And she followed the evil ways of her mother. When Jehoram died, his son Ahaziah became king. He was also a wicked king.

Because of their evil ways, God was going to allow the king of Syria to punish Israel and Judah.

God's Judgment on Wicked Men

2 Kings 9:1–29

During the time that Elisha was prophet in Israel, Hazael became king of Syria. And Jehu became king of Israel. Elisha sent a young prophet to tell Jehu that when he became king he was to destroy the whole family of Ahab.

Ahaziah, king of Judah, decided to go to Jezreel to visit Joram, the king of Israel. Joram was King Ahaziah's uncle, and he was sick. He had been wounded in battle with Hazael, king of Syria. While Ahaziah and Joram were together, Jehu started out to take over the kingdom of Israel.

A watchman in the tower at Jezreel sent a message to the king. He said, "I see a group of men coming."

King Joram said, "Send a man on horseback and ask them, 'Are you coming in peace?' "

The horseman went. But when they met, Jehu answered, "What do you have to do with peace? Follow behind me."

The watchman told the king, "The horseman met them, but he does not come back."

The king sent out another messenger to meet them. The messenger said, "The king asks, 'Are you coming in peace?'"

Again Jehu answered, "What do you have to do with peace? Follow behind me."

The watchman reported to King Joram again, "The messenger met them, but he did not come back. The man drives like Jehu, for he drives furiously."

When King Joram heard that, he decided to go meet the group of men himself. Ahaziah, king of Judah, went with him. They met the men at the piece of land that had belonged to Naboth.

Joram called, "Is it peace?"

Jehu replied, "How can there be peace when your mother, Jezebel, does such wicked things?"

When Joram heard these words he turned and fled. He warned Ahaziah, "Jehu has not come peacefully."

Jehu drew his bow and arrow. With all his strength, he shot an arrow through Joram. King Joram sank down in his chariot. Jehu said to his captain, "Throw him into the field of Naboth. For remember how Ahab, his father, had innocent

Naboth killed. Because of this, throw the body of Joram, Ahab's son, into the field that was Naboth's."

When Ahaziah saw what happened, he tried to get away. But Jehu followed him. He commanded his servants to kill Ahaziah, which they did.

Remember that the Lord had said Jehu was to destroy all the wicked house of Ahab. Ahaziah's mother was the daughter of Ahab, so Ahaziah was Ahab's grandson.

Lesson 3

Ahab's Wicked House Destroyed

2 Kings 9:30–10:17

Jehu went on to Jezreel. When Jezebel heard about it, she painted her face and looked out her window from the second floor. As Jehu entered the gate, she called to him.

Jehu looked up and saw her. He called, "Who is on my side? Who?"

Several men looked out the window. Jehu cried, "Throw her down." So they threw Jezebel out the window. Some of her blood sprinkled on the wall and on the horses, and she was trampled under their feet.

Jehu went in and ate and drank. A little while later he said to the men, "Go out and bury this cursed woman because she is a king's daughter."

The men obeyed him and went. They soon returned and said, "We found her skull, her feet, and the palms of her hands." That was all they could find of her body.

Jehu reminded them that this is what the Lord had said by His prophet Elijah: "The dogs shall eat the flesh of Jezebel."

The Lord wanted everyone in Ahab's household to be destroyed because they were so wicked.

Ahab had seventy sons living in Samaria. Jehu wrote letters to the men who raised Ahab's children. He told them to make one of Ahab's sons king and to defend themselves. When they received the letters, they were very much afraid. They had heard that Jehu had already killed two kings. The ruler of Ahab's house sent word back, "We are your servants. We will do whatever you say."

Jehu sent them another letter saying, "If you will do what I say, then take the heads off the seventy sons of Ahab and bring them to me by this time tomorrow." As soon as they received this letter, they killed the seventy sons and put their heads in baskets and sent them to Jehu.

In the morning Jehu talked to the people. He said, "Everything that the Lord has said by Elijah is surely going to happen. All of Ahab's wicked house will be destroyed." This included all his relatives, his priests, and his great men.

Jehu started out to go to Samaria. On the way he met a group of men. He asked, "Who are you?"

They answered, "We are the brothers of King Ahaziah." They were the grandsons of Ahab and Jezebel.

Jehu commanded his servants to kill them. Altogether there were forty-two men. Jehu was determined to get rid of all that remained of the house of Ahab.

Lesson 4

The Worshipers of Baal Destroyed

2 Kings 10:18–11:8

Jehu called all the people of Israel together. He said to them, "Ahab served Baal a little, but Jehu shall serve him much. I have a great sacrifice to make to Baal. All who serve Baal, come to me."

In this way he tricked the people. They did not know that his plan was to get them all together so that he could destroy all who worshiped Baal.

Everyone who served Baal came to the house of Baal. There was not one who did not come. The house of Baal was full from one end to the other.

Jehu called the man who had charge of the clothing. He said, "Bring out clothes for all who worship Baal." Then the crowd was searched to make sure that no one who served God was there.

The worshipers of Baal offered sacrifices and burnt offerings. Jehu had appointed eighty men to kill all who worshiped Baal. They stood on the outside. Jehu said, "Do not let one escape. If you do, you will be killed for the one you let get away."

When the Baal worshipers finished their offerings, the eighty men went in and killed them. They threw them out of the house of Baal. They took the images out and burned them, and broke down the house of Baal.

That is how Jehu destroyed the worship of Baal in Israel. God told Jehu that he had done well in this and in destroying the house of wicked Ahab. He said, "Because you have obeyed Me in this, I will reward you." God promised to let four generations of Jehu's sons be kings in Israel.

But Jehu was not careful to obey the Lord in everything. He sinned, and the people of Israel sinned. Because of this, the Lord allowed Hazael, king of Syria, to come and kill many people in Israel.

Jehu died after he had reigned over Israel for twenty-eight years.

In Judah, after King Ahaziah had been killed, his mother Athaliah decided to be queen. She quickly destroyed all the king's sons but one.

Ahaziah had a sister who was the wife of Jehoiada the priest. She took little Joash, the only son of King Ahaziah who was left alive, and hid him in a bedroom. Then Athaliah could not find him to kill him. He was about one year old.

For six years Joash was hid in the house of the Lord. His uncle Jehoiada, the good priest, taught him in the way of the lord. During this time wicked Athaliah reigned as queen over the land.

When Joash was about seven years old, Jehoiada the priest brought him out. He called the rulers, captains, and guards together. He brought them into the house of the Lord. There he showed them Joash, who had been hidden all those years. He felt that the time had come that Joash should be king in the place of wicked Queen Athaliah. He told the people his plans. And he told them what they should do. He said, "Joash is a descendant of good King David. He should rule Judah because the Lord chose David's descendants to be our rulers."

Many of the men in Judah agreed. But Jehoiada knew there would be some who would not like this and would try to kill Joash.

So he divided the men into three groups. One group was to guard the king's house. One was to guard the gate, and the other group was to stay behind the guards. Jehoiada wanted to protect Joash. And if anyone came inside the temple, the guards were to kill him.

Joash, the Boy King

2 Kings 11:9–12:16; 2 Chronicles 23:1–24:14

The men of Judah obeyed Jehoiada. He gave them the spears and shields of David that were in the temple. He said, "Let no one go into the temple except the priests." They stood around and guarded the temple very carefully.

Jehoiada brought out Joash and put the crown on him. He anointed him king. The people clapped their hands and shouted, "God save the king!"

Queen Athaliah saw the crowd of people. She heard the shouts of joy. She rushed into the temple. There she saw little Joash, the son of Ahaziah, standing in the temple. The people had crowned him king, and she did not like it. She tore her clothes and cried, "Treason, treason!"

Jehoiada commanded the captains and officers to take her outside, because the priests said, "Do not slay her in the temple."

He told them to kill both her and anyone who followed her.

Then Jehoiada made an agreement between the Lord and little King Joash. He also made an agreement between the king and the people. The agreement was that they should belong to the Lord.

Little seven-year-old Joash was not old enough yet to know how to rule the people. So until he grew up to be a man, his uncle Jehoiada helped him. He taught Joash how to be a good ruler. He taught him to love and serve God. Joash was wise enough to obey Jehoiada. All the people rejoiced.

They broke down the house of Baal and all the altars and images.

Joash wanted to repair the temple of the Lord, which had been broken down. He said to the priests, "Go out into the cities of Judah and gather money from all Israel to repair the house of the Lord from year to year. Hurry and do this!"

The Levites did not do this work quickly, as Joash had commanded. The king asked Jehoiada the high priest, "Why have you not started the repairing of the temple?"

So Jehoiada took a chest and bored a hole in it. He set the chest beside the altar in the house of the Lord. The priests put into the chest all the money which the people brought. The people were glad to give money to help in the work of the Lord. And soon there was much money in the chest. The collection was given to the men who had charge of repairing the temple. They used this money to pay the workers for the needed repairs. No one kept a record of how much money was spent, because the men were faithful. They could be trusted to spend the money wisely.

When they finished repairing the house of the Lord, there was some money left over. They brought what was left and gave it to Jehoiada. He used this money to make vessels of silver and gold to be dedicated to the house of the Lord. For the wicked sons of Athaliah had taken the holy vessels out of the temple of the Lord and put them in the temples of Baal.

Lesson 6

The Sad End of Joash

2 Kings 12:17–15:1; 2 Chronicles 24:15–26:1

Jehoiada lived to be one hundred thirty years old. As long as the good priest lived, Joash served the Lord. When Jehoiada died, the people honored him as a king. They buried him among the kings. They did this because he had done so much good in Israel.

After the death of the good priest, Joash let the princes of Judah persuade him not to serve the true God. He began to worship idols. The Lord sent prophets to warn him to turn back to the Lord. But he would not listen.

Then the Spirit of the Lord came upon Zechariah, the son of the good priest Jehoiada. He said, "The Lord asks, 'Why do you disobey the commandments of the Lord?' When you do this, you cannot prosper. Because you have forsaken the Lord, He has forsaken you."

King Joash would not listen to Zechariah, the son of Jehoiada. He commanded that he be stoned. He did not remember all the kindness that

263

Jehoiada had done to him.

The Lord could not bless Joash now. He allowed the Syrians to come up and fight with Judah. The Syrian army was small. Yet they were able to kill many of the people of Judah. Because they had turned away from God, God would not help them.

When the Syrians left, Joash was very sick. Then his own servants killed him on his bed. They buried him in the city of David but not with the kings. His son Amaziah became king in his place.

The prophet Elisha became very sick. Before he died, Jehoash, the king of Israel, came to see him, He wept and said, "O my father, my father." Elisha must have seemed like a father to him. Elisha said to him, "Take bow and arrows," and he took them.

Elisha said, "Put your hand upon the bow," and he put his hand upon it. Then Elisha put his hands upon the king's hands.

Elisha said, "Open the window toward the east." After the king opened the window, Elisha said, "Shoot." The king shot. Elisha told the king that he would smite the Syrians in Aphek until he destroyed them.

Then Elisha told Jehoash to take some arrows

and hit the ground. The king hit the ground three times. Elisha was displeased that he had hit the ground only three times. He said, "You should have hit the ground many times. Then you would have smitten the Syrians until you destroyed them. But now you will smite them only thrice."

Soon after this, Elisha died. He was buried in a cave.

One time some men were taking a man out to bury him. As they were burying him, they spied a band of men. Quickly they threw the dead man into the same grave where Elisha was buried. When the man touched the bones of Elisha, he came to life! How surprised they must have been when the man whom they were going to bury stood up on his feet!

There were many different kings in Israel. Although none of them were good kings, yet the Lord was merciful to Israel. Because of His promise to Abraham, Isaac, and Jacob, God did not destroy them. But He often punished them because of their sin.

Most of Judah's kings were not as wicked as Israel's kings. Some of them obeyed the Lord. There were always some people in Judah who were faithful to the Lord.

God always had faithful prophets to warn Israel and Judah.

Lesson 7

Uzziah and Isaiah

2 Chronicles 26; 27; Isaiah 6

Sixteen-year-old Uzziah became king of Judah in the place of his father Amaziah. He was the grandson of Joash. Uzziah tried to obey the Lord as long as Zechariah was prophet. While he obeyed God, God helped him. He made things go well for him. Uzziah broke down the walls of the enemies. He built towers. He made engines. He dug wells. He had many vineyards. He prepared shields and weapons of war for his large army. People from far and near heard about Uzziah. God had helped him to become great.

But when Uzziah became strong, he became proud and disobeyed the Lord. He went into the temple to burn incense on the altar, which no one but the priests were supposed to do. The priests went in to him and warned him that he should not do this.

Eighty-one of the Lord's priests went in after him. They tried to stop him. They said, "Only the sons of Aaron are to burn incense. Go out, because you have sinned."

Uzziah became very angry. While he was angry with the priests, the Lord smote him with leprosy.

The priests looked at Uzziah and saw the leprosy in his forehead. Quickly they cast him out of the temple. Uzziah himself hurried to get out because the Lord had smitten him.

Now King Uzziah was a leper. He could no longer live among his people. He had to live in a separate house the rest of his life. When he died, he was buried with the kings in the city of David.

Jotham, Uzziah's son, became king after his father died. We do not know much about Jotham except that he obeyed the Lord.

In the same year that King Uzziah died, Isaiah was a prophet in Israel. He had a wonderful vision. He saw the Lord sitting on a throne in the temple. Heavenly beings stood above the throne. Each one had six wings. With two wings he covered his face. With two wings he covered his feet. And with two wings he flew. One called to another and said, "Holy, holy, holy is the Lord of hosts. The whole earth is full of His glory."

When the heavenly beings spoke, the posts of the door moved and the house filled with smoke.

When Isaiah saw the strange and wonderful things, he realized how sinful he was. God is so pure and holy that Isaiah felt very sinful. He said, "Woe is me! for I am undone. I am a man of unclean lips. I live among a people of unclean lips. My eyes have seen the King, the Lord of hosts."

Then one of the heavenly beings flew to Isaiah. In his hand he carried a burning coal. He had taken it with tongs from off the altar. He laid it on Isaiah's mouth and said, "This has touched your lips. Your sin is taken away."

Then Isaiah heard the Lord say, "Whom shall I send? Who will go for us?"

Isaiah answered, "Here am I; send me."

The Lord said to Isaiah, "Go." He told him what to say.

Isaiah wrote a book in the Old Testament. In the Book of Isaiah he tells about Jesus and His work on the earth. The fifty-third chapter is a beautiful story about Jesus' redemptive work. It tells about His suffering and what He was willing to go through for us so that we could be saved. Isaiah wrote these things about seven hundred years before Jesus was born in Bethlehem.

Ahaz and Hezekiah

2 Kings 16; 2 Chronicles 28; 29:1–19

After Jotham died, his son Ahaz became king of Judah. He was a wicked king. He did as the wicked kings of Israel and as the heathen around him. He made images and burned incense. He even burned his own children in the fire. Because of his great wickedness, God allowed the king of Syria and the king of Israel to fight against Judah and take them captive.

A prophet of the Lord came to the king of Israel. He said, "The Lord allowed you to capture Judah because they sinned." He reminded Israel that the Lord was angry with Israel, too, because of their sins. He said, "Let the people of Judah go back to their homes, for they are your brothers."

The rulers of the people listened to the prophet. They decided they would not allow any more captives to be brought. They gave shoes and clothes to all the captives who needed them. They gave them something to eat and drink. They decided to take them back to their homes. They put all the feeble ones on donkeys to ride back to the land of Judah.

King Ahaz should have learned from this experience to fear God. But he kept on sinning against the Lord. He sinned more by offering sacrifices to the gods of the Syrians. He said, "Because the gods of the kings of Syria help them, I will sacrifice to them so that they will help me." Of course they did not help him. Idols can never help anyone.

Ahaz shut the doors of the temple of the Lord and destroyed the vessels in it. He made many altars to heathen gods. While he reigned, Judah was in great distress.

When Ahaz died, he was not buried with the kings. His son, Hezekiah, reigned in his place. Hezekiah's reign began at a time when Judah was in great trouble.

Hezekiah did not follow in the wicked ways of his father. He did that which was right in the sight of the Lord. His mother was the daughter of the good prophet Zechariah. She must have taught him to love and obey the true God.

In the first year of his reign, Hezekiah opened the doors of the house of the Lord which his father had closed. He gathered the priests and the Levites together and said, "Listen to me. Sanctify yourselves and clean up the house of the God of your fathers. Carry all the filthiness out of this holy place, for our fathers have sinned. They have forsaken the Lord. They have shut the doors to the Lord's house and have put out the lamps. They have not offered burnt offerings to God. That is why the Lord's anger is coming on Judah. He has allowed great trouble to come on us as you can see with your own eyes. Our fathers have been killed with the sword. Our children and our wives have been taken captive. All this has happened because we have turned away from the Lord.

"Now it is in my heart to make a promise to the Lord God of Israel so that He will not be angry with us any longer. My sons, do not neglect your duty. The Lord has chosen you to stand before Him, to serve Him, and to burn incense."

The priests and the Levites obeyed King Hezekiah. First they sanctified themselves; then they cleaned the house of the Lord. They carried out all the dirt and filthiness and threw it into the brook Kidron. In sixteen days they finished their cleaning job.

Then they reported to Hezekiah, "We have

cleansed all the house of the Lord. We have cleansed the altar and the shewbread table with all the vessels. All the vessels which King Ahaz threw away in his sin are put back before the altar of the Lord."

Judah Worships the Lord

2 Chronicles 29–31

There was great rejoicing in Judah. Good King Hezekiah loved and served the true God. He had opened the doors to the house of the Lord that his father had closed.

King Hezekiah gathered the rulers of the city together. They went up to the house of the Lord. They brought seven bullocks, seven rams, seven lambs, and seven he goats for a sin offering.

Hezekiah told the priest to offer them to the Lord on the altar. He commanded that a sin offering be made for all Israel. The priests killed the animals. They caught the blood and sprinkled it on the altar.

First they offered the sin offering. After that Hezekiah commanded the priests to offer a burnt offering. When the burnt offering began, the singers began to sing the song of the Lord. All the people worshiped God. The singers kept on singing, and trumpets were blown until the burnt offering was finished.

What a time of rejoicing that was! The king and all the people bowed their heads and worshiped. The Levites sang psalms and praises with gladness. They bowed their heads and worshiped. Hezekiah said, "Now you have given yourselves to the Lord. Come and bring sacrifices and thank offerings to the house of the Lord." The people brought so many animals that there were not enough priests to get all the animals ready for the burnt offerings. So other Levites helped with the priests' work. The king and all the people rejoiced that the Lord had helped them.

King Hezekiah wrote letters to warn the people to turn again to God. He sent men to carry the letters to all the people of Israel and Judah. He wanted to invite everyone to come and keep the Passover at the house of the Lord. It had been a long time since they had kept the Passover as they were commanded.

Hezekiah's letter said:

Ye children of Israel,

Do not be like your fathers and like your brethren who sinned against the Lord. Because of this, He has left them, as you see. Now do not be stubborn as your fathers were. Yield yourselves to the Lord. Enter into His sanctuary, which He has made holy forever. Serve the Lord so that He will not be angry with you any more. If you turn to the Lord, those who have taken your brothers and children captive will have compassion on them. They will let them come again into this land. The Lord your God is gracious and merciful. He will not turn away from you if you return to Him.

The king's messengers went from city to city. They carried the letters throughout the lands of Israel and Judah. Some people in Israel laughed at them. Some made fun of them. Others humbled themselves and came to Jerusalem to keep the Passover. But in Judah all the people were glad to obey the Lord and the king.

When they kept the Passover, there was great joy in Jerusalem. There had not been anything like it since the days of King Solomon, the son of David.

There was no king in Judah like Hezekiah, before him or after him. He trusted the Lord and did not depart from Him. He followed and obeyed Him. The Lord was with Hezekiah and helped him wherever he went.

Trouble in Israel

2 Kings 17; 18; 2 Chronicles 32:1–15; Isaiah 36

At the time that good King Hezekiah reigned in Judah, Hoshea was king of Israel. He was the last king in Israel. Altogether Israel had nineteen kings, and none of them were good. They had forsaken the Lord and would not obey Him. They worshiped idols and followed after many heathen ways. God had sent prophets to warn them, "Turn from your evil ways and keep my commandments." But they would not listen.

Now God was going to allow their kingdom to be destroyed. They would no longer be a separate nation.

The king of Assyria was coming with his army. He had already destroyed many other cities. He had taken many people captive. He came and fought against Samaria, the capital of Israel. He took the people captive into heathen countries.

After this the king of Assyria attacked Judah. King Hezekiah sent word to him. He promised to give him what he asked if only he would leave. The king of Assyria asked for much gold and silver. Hezekiah gave all that could be found in the king's house and in the house of the Lord. In order to get enough, he even cut off the gold that was put over the doors and the pillars of the temple.

The king of Assyria received his money. Yet he did not let Judah alone. He sent Rabshakeh with a large army to Jerusalem. Hezekiah sent out three of his men to talk to him.

Rabshakeh said to them, "Tell Hezekiah that the great king, the king of Assyria, asks, 'In what is your confidence? In whom are you trusting? You say you are strong enough for war, but these are worthless words.' The king wants to know in whom you trust that you rebel against him." Rabshakeh wanted to make the people of Judah feel afraid. He tried to make them feel weak in comparison to the Assyrians. He even said that the Lord had told him to come up and destroy the land of Judah.

Rabshakeh spoke to them in the Jews' language. The three men whom King Hezekiah sent out said, "Please speak to us in the Syrian language. We can understand it. Do not speak in the Jews' language." They did not want the people to hear what the Assyrians were saying.

Rabshakeh answered, "Has my master sent me to speak to you and to your master? Has he not sent me to speak to the men who sit on the wall?" Rabshakeh spoke in the Jews' language on purpose so all the people could understand. He wanted to make them afraid. He cried to them in a loud voice. He said, "The king says, 'Do not let Hezekiah deceive you. He will not be able to deliver you out of my hand. Do not think that the Lord can deliver you and your city out of the hand of the king of Assyria. Do not listen to Hezekiah. Do not let him persuade you that the Lord will help you. Have any of the gods of the other nations been able to deliver them out of my hand? Who, among all the gods of the countries, has been able to deliver his country out of my hand? Do not think that the Lord can deliver you and Jerusalem out of my hand.'

"The king of Assyria says, 'Make an agreement with me, and I will be good to you and give you everything you need. I will give you a good land like your own. You can eat your own food. You will live and not die. Do not listen to Hezekiah or think the Lord can help you.'"

The people kept still. They did not answer Rabshakeh's questions. Hezekiah, their king, had commanded them, "Do not answer Rabshakeh."

The Proud Assyrians
Are Destroyed

2 Kings 19; Isaiah 37

Rabshakeh had tried to frighten the people of
Judah. The three men whom Hezekiah had sent
to Rabshakeh came back to Hezekiah. They had
their clothes torn. They told him what Rabshakeh
had said. When King Hezekiah heard what they
said, he tore his clothes. He covered himself with
sackcloth and went into the house of the Lord.
He sent some men to Isaiah the prophet. They
went, clothed in sackcloth, and told Isaiah what
Rabshakeh had said against God. "Please pray
for us," they said.

Isaiah said, "Tell the king that the Lord says,
'Do not be afraid of the words of the king of
Assyria. I will cause him to hear a rumor. He will
go back to his own land. There he will fall by the
sword.'"

Rabshakeh went back to his land. Soon the
king of Assyria sent him to Hezekiah with a letter.

The letter said:

> Do not let the God in whom you trust deceive you. Do not think that God can save Jerusalem out of the hand of the king of Assyria. You have heard what the kings of Assyria have done to all the lands. They have destroyed them! And how shall you be delivered? Have any of the gods of the nations delivered them?

When Hezekiah read the letter, he went up to the house of the Lord. He spread the letter before the Lord. Then he prayed, saying, "O Lord God of Israel, You are the God, even You alone, of all the kingdoms of the earth. You have made heaven and earth. Lord, bow down Your ear and hear. Open Your eyes and see. Hear the words of the king of Assyria.

"It is true, Lord, the kings of Assyria have destroyed other lands. They have thrown their gods into the fire because they were no gods. They were only wood and stone. They were made of men's hands; that is why they could be destroyed.

"Now because of this, O Lord God, please save us out of his hand. Save us so that all the kingdoms of the earth will know that You are the Lord God, even You only."

Isaiah the prophet told Hezekiah, "God has

heard your prayer. He says the king of Assyria will not come to Jerusalem or shoot an arrow there. God has promised to defend the city. He will save it for His Name's sake and for the sake of His people."

That night the angel of the Lord went to the camp of the Assyrians. He slew 185,000 Assyrians. All the king's captains and great men were killed.

The king of Assyria had talked very proudly about his greatness. He had talked against the Lord. But the Lord proved that He was much greater. He turned the king of Assyria back to his own land in shame.

Soon after this he was worshiping in the house of his god, and his sons came in and killed him.

Hezekiah's Last Days

2 Kings 20; 2 Chronicles 32:24–33; Isaiah 38; 39

King Hezekiah was deathly sick. The prophet Isaiah came to visit him. He said to the king, "Set your house in order because you are going to die."

Hezekiah did not want to die. He wanted to live. He turned his face toward the wall and prayed to God. He said, "Please, Lord, remember now how I have obeyed You. I have done what is right in Your sight." Hezekiah wept greatly.

Isaiah left the king, but before he had gone very far, God spoke to him. He said, "Go back to Hezekiah, the captain of My people. Tell him I have heard his prayer and seen his tears. I will heal him. In three days, he shall go to the house of the Lord. I will let him live fifteen years longer. I will also deliver him and the city of Jerusalem out of the hand of the king of Assyria."

Isaiah returned to Hezekiah with God's message. He asked for a lump of figs to be laid on the king's boil so he would be healed.

Hezekiah asked Isaiah for a sign from the

Lord so he could know that the Lord would do all this for him. He wanted to know that he would be healed and that he could go to the house of the Lord on the third day.

Isaiah gave Hezekiah a choice of two signs. Both of them were signs on the sundial. He could ask that the shadow on the sundial go forward ten degrees or backward ten degrees.

Hezekiah thought about it. He answered, "It is nothing unusual for the shadow to go forward ten degrees. No, let the shadow go backward ten degrees." That would indeed be very strange. Such a thing had never happened before. The sun always rises in the east. It moves across the sky and sets in the west. It never goes backward. If this would happen, Hezekiah would know the sign was from the Lord.

Isaiah prayed to the Lord. He asked God to do this thing for Hezekiah. And God brought the shadow on the sundial backward ten degrees.

Hezekiah recovered from his sickness. But he was not thankful as he should have been. He became proud.

The prince of Babylon sent Hezekiah a present when he heard that he had been sick. King Hezekiah was pleased to see the messengers who brought it. He showed them all his treasures. There was nothing he did not show them.

Isaiah the prophet came to Hezekiah again. He asked, "What did these men say, and from where did they come?"

Hezekiah answered, "They came from Babylon."

"What did they see in your house?" asked Isaiah.

Hezekiah answered, "They have seen everything that is in my house. I showed them all my treasures."

Isaiah said, "Listen to what the Lord says. The days are coming in which everything that is in your house will be taken away from you. All that is in your house which your fathers have laid up will be carried into Babylon. Nothing shall be left."

This happened to Hezekiah because he had become proud. But Hezekiah humbled himself before the Lord. When he died, he was buried in the best of the sepulchers of the sons of David. He was greatly honored because he had done much good in Judah.

God's Judgment and Mercy

2 Kings 21; 2 Chronicles 33

Manasseh, the son of Hezekiah, reigned in the place of his father. He was a very wicked king. He was much more like his grandfather Ahaz than like his godly father, Hezekiah. He built altars to Baalim. He made his children pass through fire. He used witchcraft. He made the people of Judah do wicked things. He killed many innocent people. He made an idol and set it up in the house of the Lord.

Many years before this, God had made a promise to David and to Solomon. He said, "In this house I will put My Name forever. My mercy will not depart from Judah. I will be a father to him, and he shall be my son. If he sins, I will punish him."

The Lord sent prophets to speak to Manasseh. They warned him of the punishment that would come. Judah had sinned greatly, and God would bring much evil on them. He said He would wipe Jerusalem as a man wipes a dish—wiping it and turning it upside-down.

Manasseh did not heed the warning of the prophets. Because of this, the Lord allowed the Assyrians to come down and fight against him. They bound Manasseh with chains, and they carried him away to Babylon.

When he was in trouble, Manasseh thought about the Lord. He humbled himself and prayed to the Lord for help. The Lord was good to Manasseh. He heard his prayer and brought him back to Jerusalem. Then Manasseh knew that the Lord is God. He took away the idols out of the house of the Lord. He got rid of all the altars he had built at Jerusalem. He repaired the altar of the Lord and sacrificed to the Lord. He commanded Judah to serve the Lord God of Israel.

God did not forget His promise: "My mercy will not depart from Judah. I will be a father to him, and he shall be My son." When Manasseh turned from his sins and obeyed the Lord, God remembered and blessed him.

After Manasseh died, his son Amon became king. He was as wicked as his father had been. But he did not humble himself as Manasseh had done. He sinned more and more. His servants killed him in his own house. Remember that when God said, "My mercy will not depart from Judah," He also said, "If he sins, I will punish him."

The people of the land killed the men who had killed the king. They made Amon's son, Josiah, king in his place.

Josiah was only eight years old when he was made king.

Lesson 14

The Good Reign of Josiah

2 Kings 22:1–23:30; 2 Chronicles 34; 35

When young Josiah was sixteen, he began to seek after God. He tried to do what God wanted him to do.

When he was twenty years old, he cleaned up Judah and Jerusalem. He destroyed the images and the altars of Baalim. He ground the images to dust. He scattered the dust on the graves of those who had sacrificed to idols. He burned the bones of the priests on the altar. By doing this, he cleansed Judah and Jerusalem.

After this he sent some men to repair the house of the Lord. While these men were at work, the high priest found the Book of the Law in the house of the Lord. The high priest gave it to one of the scribes to read. After the scribe had read it, he brought it to the king and read it to him.

When King Josiah heard the words of the Book, he tore his clothes. The Book told of God's anger against them. God was angry because of the sins of their fathers. They had disobeyed the

Lord. The king asked the priest to go and ask the Lord about this.

He went and asked the Lord. God answered, "I will do as it is written because Judah has forsaken the Lord." But He promised that He would not do it in the days of Josiah. Josiah had obeyed the Lord; therefore he would die peacefully. He would not see the evil that God would bring on the people of Judah.

King Josiah sent for the older men of Judah and Jerusalem. He went up into the house of the Lord. The priests, the prophets, and all the people gathered together there. Josiah read to them the words of the Law which had been found in the house of God.

The king stood by a pillar. He promised the Lord they would obey the words which were written in the Book. The people agreed to do what the king said.

Josiah was careful to keep his promise. He destroyed the idols in the land of Judah. He also cleaned up the land of Samaria and Israel. He got rid of the altars. He cut down the groves where the people worshiped idols. He broke down the altar that had been made by Jeroboam, the first king of Israel after the kingdoms were divided.

As Josiah turned around, he saw the sepulchers in the mountain. He had the bones of the dead men brought out of them and burned on the altar.

Do you remember the story of the man of God who had come to Bethel when Jeroboam was standing by the altar to burn incense? The man of God had said a man named Josiah would be born who would burn the bones of the priests who had sacrificed on that altar. For a sign that this would happen, the altar had been broken and the ashes poured out. Now his prophecy was being fulfilled. King Josiah noticed a title on one of the sepulchers. He asked what it said. The men of the city told him, "This is the sepulcher of the man of God. He prophesied of the things that you are doing now."

Josiah said, "Let him alone. Do not let anyone move his bones."

The king returned to Jerusalem. He commanded the people to keep the Feast of the Passover. It was written in the Book of the Law that it should be kept.

There was no king before or after Josiah who turned to the Lord more than he did. Josiah followed the Lord with all his heart, with all his soul, and with all his might.

When Josiah died, he was taken to Jerusalem. There he was buried in one of the sepulchers of his fathers.

Daniel Dares to Do Right

2 Kings 23:31–24:1–6; 2 Chronicles 36:1–8; Daniel 1

After Josiah died, his son Jehoahaz began to reign in his place. He reigned only three months. Then the king of Egypt came and took him down to Egypt, where he died.

The king of Egypt made Jehoiakim, his brother, king in his place. The king of Egypt commanded him to tax the people. This tax money was to be paid to the king of Egypt.

Because Jehoiakim was a wicked king, the Lord punished him. He allowed Nebuchadnezzar, king of Babylon, to fight against Jerusalem. Nebuchadnezzar tried to take possession of it. He took vessels out of the house of the Lord. He put them in the house of his god. King Jehoiakim and many others were taken captive.

Day after day the captives walked. Every day they were getting farther and farther away from their homes. King Nebuchadnezzar and his men were taking the Jews to Babylon. The king wanted to use some of these captives to help him in his kingdom.

The Jewish captives spoke the Hebrew language. The people in Babylon spoke the Chaldean language. The king wanted the chosen men to be able to talk his language. It would not be good to have people working for him who could not understand and speak his language. He knew it would be easier to teach young people a new language than to teach the older ones. So the king told his helpers to bring in good, healthy young people. He wanted people who were wise and could learn his language.

Some of the young men chosen were Daniel, Hananiah, Mishael, and Azariah. The king changed their names. He called Daniel, Belteshazzar. He called Hananiah, Shadrach. He called Mishael, Meshach, and Azariah, Abednego. He wanted Daniel and his three friends to drink wine and eat special food each day. They were to be on the king's diet for three years. He hoped that by the end of three years they would be ready to work in his palace.

Daniel knew it would be wrong to drink wine. He knew it would be wrong to eat the king's meat. God had given the children of Israel some laws about what foods they were not to eat. The people of other nations did not obey God's laws. They ate meats that God said were not to be eaten. They drank wine.

Daniel was determined not to defile himself with these things. He asked one of the princes to excuse him from eating anything that would not be pleasing to God.

God caused the prince to love Daniel very much, and he did not want to make Daniel do something wrong. But he was afraid not to do as the king had commanded. He was afraid that when Daniel and his friends would come before the king, they would not look as healthy as the others. Then he would be in trouble. He might even be beheaded for not obeying the king's orders. He explained his problem to Daniel.

Daniel went to Melzar, whom the prince had put in charge over him and his three friends. He said to Melzar, "Test your servants, I beg of you, for ten days. Let them give us vegetables to eat and water to drink. Then look at our faces and the faces of those who eat the king's meat and deal with us according to that."

Melzar consented to try this plan. At the end of ten days he could see a difference in Daniel and his friends. Their faces were fatter than the faces of the other young men. They looked healthier than all those who ate the king's meat. So Melzar took away the food and wine that the king had appointed for them. Instead he gave them only vegetables to eat and water to drink.

God blessed Daniel and his three friends with great wisdom. They were able to learn the Chaldean language and to understand many difficult things.

After three years, the king ordered, "Bring the young men to me." The king talked with them and asked them hard questions. He found Daniel and his three friends ten times better and wiser than all the wise men in his kingdom.

Lesson 16

The Wise Men of Babylon
in Danger

Daniel 2:1–24

One night King Nebuchadnezzar woke up. His thoughts troubled him because he had dreamed a strange dream. He was so disturbed that he could not go back to sleep. But when morning came, he could not remember what he had dreamed.

King Nebuchadnezzar called for his wise men. They came and stood before him. The king said, "I have dreamed a dream, and I am troubled to know what it means."

"Tell us your dream," they said. "Then we will tell you the meaning of it."

The king became very angry. He suspected that his men were not so wise after all. They could not tell him what he had dreamed, and they probably could not give the right meaning to his dream either. Probably they had just been making up things to tell him at other times. "You have been lying to me!" he accused them. "Tell me the dream; then I will know that you can show the meanings of dreams."

The troubled men cried, "There is not a man on earth who can do what you are asking. There has never been a king who has asked such a thing. No one can show the king this thing except the gods, who do not live with men."

In his rage the king commanded that all the wise men in Babylon be killed. At once he sent out men to get all the wise men.

Daniel and his three friends had not yet heard what had happened. When the king's men came to kill them, Daniel and his friends did not know why they were to be killed. Daniel asked the captain, "Why are the king's orders so hasty?"

After the captain told Daniel what had happened, Daniel asked to see the king. He said to King Nebuchadnezzar, "Give me a little time, and I will show you what the dream means." The king agreed.

Daniel hurried back to his three friends and told them about it. He asked them to pray to God for help. No one on earth was wise enough to know the king's dream, but God knew about it.

Then God showed Daniel in the night what the

king had dreamed and what the dream meant. How thankful Daniel and his friends were! Daniel said, "Blessed be the Name of God for ever and ever. Wisdom and might are His. He changes the times and the seasons. He removes kings and sets them up. He gives wisdom and knowledge. He makes known secret things. I thank You and praise You, O God of my fathers. You have given me wisdom and might. You have answered my prayer and made known to me the king's dream."

Daniel went back to the captain whom the king had appointed to destroy all the wise men of Babylon. He begged, "Do not destroy the wise men of Babylon. But bring me before the king. I will show King Nebuchadnezzar his dream and what it means."

Nebuchadnezzar's Dream

Daniel 2:25–49

One of the king's captains told the king, "I have found a man among the captives of Judah who will tell you your dream."

Quickly Daniel was brought to the king. Nebuchadnezzar asked, "Can you tell me what I have dreamed and what my dream means?"

Daniel told King Nebuchadnezzar, "No man on earth can tell the secret that you want to know. But there is a God in heaven who knows all secrets. He has told me about your dream and what it means. When you went to bed, you wondered what would happen in the future. Then God showed you what would happen.

"You saw a great image that was very bright and very terrible. The head of the image was of gold. His breast and arms were of silver. His belly and thighs were of brass. His legs were of iron, and his feet were part iron and part clay. You saw a stone cut out of the mountain without hands roll against the feet of the image. The feet were broken, and the whole image fell down and broke to pieces. The pieces were fine like chaff, and the wind blew them away. Then you saw the stone become bigger until it was like a mountain that filled the whole earth. That was your dream. Now I will tell you what the dream means.

"You, O King, are king of kings. The God of heaven has given you a kingdom of power, and strength, and glory. You are the head of gold. After you, there shall be a kingdom of silver that is not as great as you are. Then a third kingdom of brass shall rule over the whole earth. The fourth kingdom shall be a kingdom of iron. At first it shall be very strong, but it shall become weaker because it shall be divided, just as iron and clay do not mix.

"Then the God of heaven shall set up His kingdom, which shall never be destroyed. It shall stand forever. It will break and destroy all other kingdoms. This is the stone that was cut out without hands which broke in pieces the clay, the iron, the brass, the silver, and the gold. The great God has made known to the king what will happen after this. The dream is true, and the meaning is sure!"

King Nebuchadnezzar fell upon his face and

worshiped Daniel. He said, "It is true that your God is a God of gods. He is a Lord of kings. He is a revealer of secrets. He revealed to you my dream."

The king made Daniel a great man in his kingdom and gave him many gifts. He made him ruler over all the wise men of Babylon.

At Daniel's request, the king made Shadrach, Meshach, and Abednego—Daniel's three friends—rulers in the land of Babylon.

Three Men Who Would Not Bow

Daniel 3:1–18

King Nebuchadnezzar made an image of gold. It was about ninety feet high. That would be about as high as a ten-story building. He set it up in the plain. Then he prepared to have a great celebration. He sent for all his great men to gather together to worship his image. He called for the princes, the governors, the captains, the judges, the treasurers, the counselors, the sheriffs, and all the rulers. They gathered together, for no one dared to disobey the king. They stood before the image which the king had set up. Among them stood Shadrach, Meshach, and Abednego.

A herald cried loudly, "O people, nations, and languages, when you hear the sound of all kinds of music, you shall fall down before the golden image. Worship the image that Nebuchadnezzar the king has set up. If you will not fall down and worship, you will be thrown into the middle of a burning fiery furnace."

The people did not want to be thrown into the

fire. They were afraid to disobey the king's orders. So when they heard the music, they fell down and worshiped the image. Shadrach, Meshach, and Abednego knew it would be wrong to worship anyone but God. Boldly they stood up among the bowing Chaldeans.

Some of the Chaldeans came to the king and accused these Jews. They said, "O King, live forever. You, O King, have made a law that every man who hears the sound of all kinds of music shall fall down and worship the golden image. You said that whoever will not fall down and worship it shall be thrown into a burning fiery furnace. There are three captives from Judah whom you have made rulers. They are Shadrach, Meshach, and Abednego. These men, O King, have not done what you said. They do not serve your gods. They refuse to worship the golden image which you have set up."

Nebuchadnezzar was furious that some men did not obey his orders. In his fury he commanded that these men be brought to him.

The three were brought before the king. He said to them, "Is it true, O Shadrach, Meshach, and Abednego, that you do not obey me? you do not serve my gods? you did not bow down and worship the golden image which I have set up? Now if you will bow down when you hear the sound of all kinds of music, and worship the image, all will be well. But if you will not worship, you will be thrown the same hour into a burning fiery furnace. And who is that God who can deliver you out of my hands?"

It seems that it was hard for the king to believe that they would disobey him. He wanted to give them another chance. Perhaps they had not understood.

Shadrach, Meshach, and Abednego answered the king, "O King, we are not worried about this. If that is what you do, our God is the one who can deliver us from the burning fiery furnace. He will deliver us out of your hand, O King. But whatever happens, we still want you to know that we will not serve your gods. We will not worship the golden image which you have set up."

Three Men Who Would Not Burn

Daniel 3:19–30

The words of Shadrach, Meshach, and Abednego made the king very angry. He was furious! His face changed because he was so angry. He commanded that the furnace be heated seven times hotter than usual. He called the most mighty men in his army. He commanded, "Bind these three men. Throw them into the burning fiery furnace."

The king's men tied strong ropes around Shadrach, Meshach, and Abednego. They were bound in their coats, hats, and other clothes. Then they were thrown into the middle of the burning fiery furnace.

Because the king was so angry, the furnace had been made exceedingly hot. It was so hot that the flames leaped out and killed the king's men who threw them into the furnace. The three men who dared to disobey the king's orders fell bound into the burning fiery furnace.

King Nebuchadnezzar was there watching. He

saw it happen. Suddenly he saw something that he could hardly believe. He arose in haste and talked to some of his men. He said, "Did we not throw three men bound into the fire?"

"Yes, O King," his men replied.

"Look!" he cried. "I see four men in the fire, and they are not bound. They are walking in the middle of the fire. They are not hurt. The fourth man looks like the Son of God."

Nebuchadnezzar came near the door of the burning fiery furnace. He said, "Shadrach, Meshach, and Abednego, you servants of the most high God, come out of the fire. Come here to me."

The three men came out of the fire.

The king's men gathered around. They wanted to see these men who would not burn. They saw that the fire had not hurt their bodies. Not one hair on their heads was singed. Their coats were not even scorched. They did not have the smell of fire on them. Only the ropes that had bound them had been burned.

Nebuchadnezzar thought he was a great king. He had asked these men, "Who is the God that can deliver you out of my hand?" Now he knew. He found that there was someone who was much greater than he. He saw that the God of Shadrach, Meshach, and Abednego was not like his gods. This God could do great and marvelous things. Nebuchadnezzar could not even make a fire that would burn His servants.

The king said, "Blessed be the God of Shadrach, Meshach, and Abednego. He has sent His angel and delivered His servants who trusted in Him. They have changed the king's word. They have yielded their bodies that they might not serve nor worship any other god except their own God. Because of this, I make a law that all people who shall speak anything against their God shall be cut into pieces. There is no other God who can deliver in this way."

The king made Shadrach, Meshach, and Abednego even greater men in his kingdom than they had been before.

Nebuchadnezzar Dreams Again

Daniel 4:1–27

Again Nebuchadnezzar had a dream. This time when he awoke he did not forget what he had dreamed. Again he sent for all the wise men of Babylon. But they did not know what the dream meant.

King Nebuchadnezzar was troubled. At last Daniel was brought before the king. The king said, "O Daniel, I know that the spirit of the holy gods is in you. No secret troubles you. Tell me the meaning of my dream."

After this Nebuchadnezzar wrote a letter to tell all the people of the earth about it. He wrote:

Nebuchadnezzar the king, unto all people; peace be unto you.

I thought it would be good to show you what the high God has done to me. How great are His signs! How mighty are His wonders! His kingdom is an everlasting kingdom.

When I was resting in my house, I saw a dream which made me afraid, and my thoughts troubled me.

I saw a tree in the middle of the earth. It was very high. It became so great it reached to heaven. Animals found shelter under its branches. The birds made nests in its branches. People came from all over the earth to eat its fruit.

Then a holy one came down from heaven and ordered, "Cut down the great tree. Cut off its branches. Shake off its leaves and scatter its fruit. Let the animals and the birds get away from it. Yet leave the stump and the roots in the earth. Let it be wet with the dew of heaven. Let his part be with the animals. Let an animal's heart be given to him. Let seven years pass like this. Then everyone will know that there is a God in heaven. He rules all the kingdoms of the earth."

When I told Daniel my dream, he was amazed and sat quietly for an hour. His thoughts troubled him, and he wondered what to do.

Then I said, "Do not be afraid. Do not let the dream or the meaning trouble you."

Daniel answered, "I wish the dream would be true about your enemies." He took courage and said, "The tree that you saw is you, O King. You have become a great king. You heard a voice ordering the tree to be cut down. This means that you will lose your kingdom. For seven years you will live like an animal in the fields. You will eat grass like an ox. You will be wet with the dew of heaven. You will live like this until you know that the Most High rules in the kingdoms of men. After you understand that God rules over all the earth, then you will live among men again, and your kingdom will be given back to you."

Then Daniel said, "O King, take my advice. Stop your sinning. Do what is right. God is a merciful God. It may be that He will give you a time of peace."

Lesson 21

The Dream Comes True

Daniel 4:28-37

Proud King Nebuchadnezzar did not take Daniel's advice. A year passed, and nothing unusual happened. Perhaps Nebuchadnezzar almost forgot about his strange dream. He became more and more proud of his great kingdom. His palace grounds were beautiful. And the city of Babylon was very famous.

One day he walked through his palace, admiring it. Proud thoughts filled his mind. He said, "Is not this the great Babylon that I have built for myself? I have built it for my power and for my glory."

God heard the king's proud words. He saw the proud heart. He was going to show King Nebuchadnezzar that he was not so great after all.

While Nebuchadnezzar was thinking these proud thoughts and saying these words, a voice from heaven said, "O King Nebuchadnezzar! The kingdom is departed from you. You will be driven from men. You shall live with the beasts of the field. You will eat grass like the oxen for seven years until you know that the Most High rules in the kingdom of men. He gives the kingdom to whomever He will."

All this happened to the king that same hour. He was driven from men and ate grass like oxen. His body was wet with the dew of heaven. His hair grew like eagles' feathers and his nails like birds' claws.

At the end of seven years, God gave the king his understanding again. Then the king lifted up his eyes to heaven and thanked God. He praised the Lord for His greatness. He said, "All the living creatures and the earth are counted as nothing before Him. He does according to His will in heaven and among those who live on the earth. No one can keep Him from doing it, or ask Him, 'What are you doing?'"

Again God heard the king's words and saw his heart. When the king honored God, God gave him back his kingdom. Now Nebuchadnezzar knew that God is greater than any man.

Nebuchadnezzar said, "Now I, Nebuchadnezzar, praise and honor the King of heaven, whose words all are truth. Those who walk in pride, He is able to humble."

After Nebuchadnezzar's death, Belshazzar, the son of Nebuchadnezzar's daughter, reigned in his place.

Lesson 22

The Lord Speaks to Jeremiah

Jeremiah 1–21

Before young Josiah was made king in Judah, the priest Hilkiah had a son. The little boy was called Jeremiah.

When Jeremiah was twenty years old, God spoke to him. He said to Jeremiah, "I want you to be My prophet." At first Jeremiah did not feel able to do this great work. He said, "O Lord God! I cannot speak; I am only a child."

The Lord said, "Do not say that. Go wherever I send you. Say whatever I command you. I will be with you. Do not be afraid."

Jeremiah obeyed the Lord. He was prophet in Judah from the days of good King Josiah until the days of the last kings of Judah.

Many times the messages which God wanted Jeremiah to tell the people were not pleasant to hear. Judah had sinned. Many of the messages were warnings of the punishment they would receive. God is faithful to give warnings to turn away from sin. But people often do not appreciate the warnings as they should.

The people of Judah saw what happened to Israel because of their sin. They were carried away captive to another land. Even though the people of Judah saw this, they did not take warning. Many people became angry at Jeremiah for the things he said.

The Lord still loved His people. He pleaded with them to return to Him and confess their sins. But Judah refused to return to God. There were many prophets at that time who falsely claimed to be prophets of God. They told the people of Judah things which were not true. They made them believe they could have peace even though they kept on sinning.

Jeremiah warned the people that these prophets were telling lies. But Judah would not listen. They liked to hear the nice things rather than the warnings. Jeremiah felt sorry for the people. He often wept because of their sins. He said, "Oh, that my head were waters, and mine eyes a fountain of tears, that I might weep day and night for my people." Because Jeremiah wept so much, he is often called the Weeping Prophet. The Book of Lamentations tells about the weepings of Jeremiah.

Jeremiah went to the Lord's house and told the people about the punishment which God was going to bring on them. The people of Jerusalem would be killed. The city would be left empty.

Pashur was a priest. He was also the chief governor in the house of the Lord. Pashur heard what Jeremiah had said, and he did not like it. He hit Jeremiah and put him in the stocks.

Jeremiah did not keep still just because Pashur punished him. He faithfully told the people what God had said. He told Pashur, "You and all who live in your house will be taken captive to Babylon. There you will die and be buried." He told him this would happen not only to him, but also to all the people to whom he had told lies.

Jeremiah Warns the People

Jeremiah 26; 35

Jeremiah was brave and courageous. He was not afraid to obey God. He knew that the prophets were often mistreated because they spoke out against sin. But he chose to follow the Lord anyway.

While Josiah was king, Jeremiah was treated kindly. After Josiah died, the people began worshiping idols again. They did not care for the true God. Jeremiah went throughout the land, preaching against the sins of the people. He reminded them of the punishment that would come. The people paid no attention.

After Josiah died, his son Jehoiakim was king of Judah. He was not a good man like his father. He worshiped idols and forsook God. Because Jeremiah warned him of the punishment of his sins, he treated him very unkindly.

God spoke to Jeremiah. He said, "Go, stand in the court of the Lord's house. Speak all the words which I command you to speak. Do not leave out one word. It may be that the people will listen and turn from their evil ways. Then I will not need to punish them for their sins.

Jeremiah spoke the words of the Lord. The priests and the prophets and all the people heard him. When Jeremiah was through speaking, they said, "You shall surely die." They all gathered together against Jeremiah. They accused him of saying bad things about them and against the temple.

The princes of Judah heard about this. They came from the palace to the house of the Lord and sat at the gate. Then the priests and the prophets said, "This man is worthy to die. He has spoken evil."

Jeremiah said to the princes and to all the people, "The Lord sent me to speak all the words which you have heard. Now obey the word of the Lord your God, and He will not bring all this evil upon you. As for me, do with me whatever seems good and right to you. But know for sure, if you kill me you will bring innocent blood upon yourselves and all the people in this city, because it is true that the Lord sent me."

Then the princes said, "This man is not worthy to die. He has spoken to us in the Name of the Lord our God."

Some of the older men got up and told stories about other times when the Lord sent word to His people through His prophets. When the people turned from their evil ways, the Lord did not bring evil on them.

The Lord helped Jeremiah, and he was not put to death.

The Lord told Jeremiah to go to the house of the Rechabites. He said, "Speak to them and bring them into the house of the Lord." There Jeremiah was to take them into one of the rooms and give them wine.

Jeremiah took the whole house of the Rechabites and brought them into one of the rooms in the temple. He set before them cups and pots full of wine and said to them, "Drink wine."

But the Rechabites said, "We will drink no wine because our father told us that neither we nor our sons should drink any wine forever. He told us not to build houses. Neither are we to sow seed or plant vineyards. We are always supposed to live in tents. In this we have obeyed our father."

After this the Lord told Jeremiah to go to Judah and Jerusalem. He said, "Tell them about the Rechabites, who are careful to obey their father." The people of Judah and Jerusalem were not like this. The Lord had often sent prophets to warn them, but they would not listen.

Jeremiah told the Rechabites that because they obeyed their father in everything there would always be a righteous man among them.

The King Tries
to Destroy God's Word

Jeremiah 36

While Jehoiakim was king, the word of the Lord came to Jeremiah again. The Lord told Jeremiah to take a roll of a book. In this roll God wanted him to write all the words which He had spoken. He was to write all the messages God had given him since he began to be a prophet. There were warnings of judgment against Israel and Judah and all the other nations. God did not want to punish them; and He said, "It may be that when they hear about the evil I plan to do to them, they will come back to Me. Then I can forgive their sin."

Jeremiah called for Baruch the scribe. He told him the words of the Lord. Baruch wrote all the words of the Lord in the roll.

After the words were written, Jeremiah said to Baruch, "I am shut up and cannot go into the house of the Lord. You go to the Lord's house on the fast day. Read this roll to the people and tell them these are the words of the Lord."

Baruch did as Jeremiah asked him to do. On the fast day he read the book to all the people. One of the men who was listening believed God's message. He hurried to the princes and told them the things Baruch had read to them.

The princes listened to his report eagerly. They sent a man to Baruch to tell him to bring the roll in his hand and come to them.

Baruch took the roll and came to them. The princes said to him, "Sit down now, and read it in our ears." So Baruch read the roll to the princes.

When they heard all these words they were afraid. They said to Baruch, "We must tell the king all these words."

The princes told Baruch to go hide himself and Jeremiah. They said, "Do not let any man know where you are." They did not know how the king would accept this message. He might become angry.

The king was in his winter house because it was cold. When the princes came with the roll there was a fire burning in the hearth before the king.

When his servant read three or four pages, the king cut that part off the roll with a knife. He threw it into the fire. The princes begged, "Do not burn the roll." But their pleading did no good. The king would not listen. He kept throwing pages into the fire until the whole roll was burned.

The king was not afraid. None of his servants seemed to be afraid. They should have feared the word of the Lord that was spoken against them. They should have repented of their sins. But they did not.

The king commanded some of his men to go and get Baruch and Jeremiah. But the Lord hid them.

After the king had burned the roll, the Lord spoke to Jeremiah again. He said, "Take another roll. Write in it all the words which were in the first book which the king burned."

Jeremiah took another roll and gave it to Baruch. Baruch wrote in the roll all the words that Jeremiah had told him before. Besides that, there were many other words added to it.

The second book was much longer than the first because it told about Jehoiakim's punishment. All the words of Jeremiah were true.

Not long after this the people of Judah were

taken captive. Many of the people were taken to be slaves, and King Jehoiakim was put into prison. When Jehoiakim died, his eight-year-old son Jehoiachin became king in Judah.

After a time Nebuchadnezzar also took Jehoiachin captive and left Josiah's son Zedekiah to be king over the people who remained at Jerusalem.

Judah's Punishment

Jeremiah 24; 27; 28

While Zedekiah was king of Judah, the Lord showed Jeremiah two baskets of figs. They were set before the temple of the Lord. One basket had very good figs in it. They were like the figs which ripen first. The figs in the other basket were so very bad that they could not be eaten.

The Lord said to Jeremiah, "What do you see, Jeremiah?"

He answered, "I see figs. The good figs are very good. The evil figs are very evil. They are so evil that they cannot be eaten."

The Lord said to him, "This is what the Lord, the God of Israel, says: 'The good figs mean that I will take notice of those who are carried away captive out of Judah. I have let them be taken captive by the Chaldeans for their good. I will bring them again to this land. I will build them and not pull them down. I will plant them and not pluck them up. I will give them a heart to know that I am the Lord. They shall be My people and

I will be their God when they shall return to Me with their whole heart.

" 'The evil figs are so evil that they cannot be eaten. This means that I will let the king of Judah be taken captive with all the rest of the people who do not turn to Me. They will be taken into all the kingdoms of the earth for their hurt. I will send the sword and famine and trouble among them. They will be destroyed.' "

God told Jeremiah to make wooden yokes for a sign that many nations would serve the king of Babylon. Jeremiah was to put one yoke on his own neck and to send the others to kings of other nations.

At this time there was a prophet named Hananiah. He came to the house of the Lord where Jeremiah was. In the presence of the priests and all the people he said to Jeremiah, "The Lord of hosts, the God of Israel, says that He has broken the yoke of the king of Babylon. Within two full years, He will bring back to Jerusalem all the vessels of the Lord's house which Nebuchadnezzar carried away to Babylon. The Lord will bring back the king of Judah. He will bring back all the captives of Judah who went into Babylon."

Jeremiah said, "Amen, the Lord do so. But listen to what I say. Many prophets before us spoke evil of many countries and great kingdoms. When the words of the prophets come true, you know that the Lord has sent them."

Hananiah took the yoke off Jeremiah's neck. He broke it and said in the presence of all the people, "The Lord says even like this He will break the yoke of Nebuchadnezzar within two years' time." The prophet Jeremiah went his way.

The Lord told him to go and talk to Hananiah. Again Jeremiah went. He said to him, "Listen now, Hananiah. The Lord has not sent you. But you make this people believe a lie. Because of this you will surely die this year." So Hananiah died that year in the seventh month, as Jeremiah had said.

Jeremiah Writes to the Captives

Jeremiah 29:1–10; 37

Jeremiah wrote a letter. He sent it to the captives in Babylon. It was a message from God. He
told them what they should do while they were
in this strange land. God wanted them to prepare
to stay in Babylon for a while. He told them to
build houses and live in them. They were to plant
gardens and eat the things they raised. God
wanted them to get married and have families.
He told them to pray for the city into which they
were taken so that it would have peace. Then they
could also enjoy peace. He warned them not to
let the prophets deceive them and not to trust in
their dreams. He told them the prophets had lied
to them. He told them that after seventy years
the Lord would let them return home again. He
would gather them from all the nations to which
He had driven them.

King Zedekiah and some of the Jews,
including Jeremiah, were still living at Jerusalem.
King Jehoiakim had been the one who burned the

roll with God's words, but Zedekiah would not listen to Jeremiah's warnings either. However, he did ask Jeremiah to pray for them. At this time Jeremiah was not shut up in prison. He went in and out among the people.

The Chaldeans came up against Jerusalem to take it. An army from Egypt came up to help the people of Jerusalem. The Chaldeans were afraid of the Egyptian army and left Jerusalem.

The Lord called Jeremiah. He told him to give this message to the king: "The people which have come to help you shall return to Egypt. The Chaldeans shall come again. They shall fight against this city and take it. They shall burn it with fire. Do not deceive yourselves by saying that the Chaldeans will depart from you. They shall not depart. Even though you had smitten their whole army and only wounded men remained, yet all of them would get up in their tents. They would burn this city with fire."

While the Chaldeans were gone for a little while, Jeremiah left Jerusalem. He wanted to go to the land of Benjamin. When he was in the gate, a captain caught him and accused him of something which was not true. The captain said that Jeremiah was going to give himself over to their enemies. Jeremiah denied it, but the captain would not listen to him. He took Jeremiah and brought him to the princes.

The princes were very angry with Jeremiah because of this thing. They hit him and put him in prison. He was put into a dungeon and had to stay there many days.

Zedekiah sent and took Jeremiah out of prison. He had him come to his house. There he secretly asked him whether there was any word from the Lord.

Jeremiah told him there was word from the Lord. He told him that he would be taken to Babylon. Jeremiah asked the king, "What have I done against you? What have I done against your servant? What have I done against this people that you have put me into prison? Where are your prophets which prophesied to you? They said the king of Babylon shall not come against you nor come against this land. Because of this, please listen, O my lord the king. Please do what I ask of you. Do not let me go back to the dungeon, because I might die there."

Zedekiah commanded that Jeremiah be put into the court of the prison. He was to be given a piece of bread every day until all the bread in the city was gone. Jeremiah stayed in the court of the prison. This was much better than being in the dungeon, where he had been.

Ebed-melech Helps Jeremiah

Jeremiah 32:1–12; 38

While Jeremiah was in the court of the prison, the Word of the Lord came to him. God told him that his uncle's son was coming to him. He would ask Jeremiah to buy a certain field.

When this man came to Jeremiah, he said, "Please buy my field. It is in the country of Benjamin. The right of the inheritance is yours. Buy it for yourself."

Jeremiah knew this word was from the Lord. So he bought the field from his uncle's son.

Jeremiah advised the people of Judah to go out and give themselves to the Chaldeans when they came again. He told them that if they did this they would live. But the people who stayed in the city would die.

The princes knew what Jeremiah had advised the people. They did not think this was good advice. They even thought Jeremiah was not saying this for the good of the people, but for their hurt. They asked the king to have Jeremiah put to death. The king said the princes could do to him as they wished.

The princes took Jeremiah and cast him into a dungeon. It was an old well in the court of the prison. This well was no longer used. There was no water in it. But there was soft, deep mud in the bottom. When Jeremiah was put into the dungeon he sank down into the mud.

Ebed-melech, a kind Ethiopian, was one of the king's servants. He heard that they had put Jeremiah into a dungeon. He was afraid Jeremiah would die down there. He told the king about it.

The king said, "Take thirty men with you. Get Jeremiah out of the dungeon before he dies." So Ebed-melech took thirty men with him. They went to the king's house and took from there some old rags which had been thrown away. Then they went to the dungeon where Jeremiah was. They let down the rags to him on ropes. Ebed-melech said, "Put these under your arms." This was to make a cushion so the ropes would not hurt him when they pulled him out. It would probably take much hard pulling, because Jeremiah had sunk down into the mud.

Jeremiah put the rags under his arms to keep the ropes from cutting him. Then the men drew him up with the ropes. They took him up out of the dungeon. Again Jeremiah stayed in the court of the prison.

King Zedekiah called for Jeremiah. He said to him, "I will ask you a thing. Hide nothing from me."

Jeremiah said to Zedekiah, "If I tell you, will you not surely put me to death? And if I tell you what to do, will you listen to me?"

The king secretly promised Jeremiah that he would not put him to death. He would not give him to the men who wanted to put him to death.

Then Jeremiah told the king the word of the Lord. He told him that if he would go out and give himself to the king of Babylon, he would live. The city would not be burned with fire. He and his house would not die. If he would not go out, then the city would be burned with fire. The Chaldean army would take the people captive. Even King Zedekiah would not be able to escape.

Zedekiah said to Jeremiah, "I am afraid of the Jews. They might deliver me to my enemies. They might make fun of me."

Jeremiah replied, "They will not deliver you. Obey, I beg of you, the voice of the Lord which I speak to you. If you do, it will be well with you and you will live." Jeremiah reminded the king again what would happen to him if he would not obey the voice of the Lord.

The king told Jeremiah, "Do not tell anyone what you have just told me. If you do not tell anyone, you shall not die." He told Jeremiah that if the princes heard that he had spoken to the king they might ask him what he had said. The king said, "Tell them that you asked me not to let you go back to the dungeon lest you die there." The king did not want Jeremiah to tell them the other things he had said.

Lesson 28

Jerusalem Is Taken
by the Chaldeans

Jeremiah 39; 40; 2 Kings 25

The princes knew that Jeremiah had spoken to the king. They wanted to know what he had said. Jeremiah told them what the king had said he should tell them if they asked. They were satisfied with his answer and did not ask him more about it. They did not find out the other things he had said to the king.

Jeremiah was still shut up in the court of the prison. The Lord sent him with a message to Ebed-melech. He said, "Jerusalem will be taken. But God will deliver you. You will not be killed, because you trusted in the Lord."

Jeremiah stayed in the court of the prison. He was there until the day that Jerusalem was taken.

The Chaldean army came once more to take the city of Jerusalem. King Zedekiah did not want to give himself up to the king of Babylon. The people did not want to give themselves up to their enemies to be slaves. They stayed in the city and kept the gates shut. Weary months passed by. The people inside the city were hungry. Jeremiah suffered with them.

At last the men of war tried to escape in the nighttime. They went out by the gate between two walls which was by the king's garden. King Zedekiah decided to slip away secretly. The Chaldean army went after the king. It was not long until they overtook him.

The Chaldeans broke down the walls of Jerusalem. They brought Zedekiah to their king. There they killed his sons before his eyes; then they put out Zedekiah's eyes. They bound him with chains of brass and took him to Babylon. Many other people were taken captive at this time.

About a month later Nebuzaradan, the servant of King Nebuchadnezzar, came to Jerusalem. He burned the house of the Lord. He burned the king's house and all the houses of Jerusalem. He broke to pieces the things of brass, silver, and gold which they found in the temple. He carried them to Babylon. The priests and officers of the king were taken to Babylon, where they were killed.

Jerusalem was in ruins. The beautiful and magnificent temple which Solomon had built was destroyed. The people of Judah were taken away from their homeland. They had to serve a heathen king. All this happened because of Judah's great wickedness. They would not listen when the prophets of the Lord spoke to them. Even when they saw that the false prophets' messages did not come true, still they did not heed the warning of the prophet Jeremiah.

After Jerusalem was taken, Nebuchadnezzar told some of his men what to do with Jeremiah. He said, "Take good care of him. Do not harm him. Do to him as he tells you."

The men took Jeremiah out of the court of the prison. The captain said to him, "The Lord your God has spoken evil upon this place. Now the Lord has done as He said. Judah has sinned against the Lord. Because they have not obeyed His voice, this thing is come upon them. Now, see, I loose you today from the chains which were upon your hand. If it seems good to you to come with me to Babylon, come. I will take good care of you. If it does not seem right to you to come with me to Babylon, stay here. See, all the land is before you. Wherever it seems good for you to go, go there." The captain gave Jeremiah food and a reward and let him go.

The king of Babylon made Gedaliah governor. He set him over the people who remained at Jerusalem. Jeremiah chose to stay there with him and the other people who were left in the land of Judah.

Lesson 29

Ishmael Deceives Gedaliah

Jeremiah 40:1–41:15

Gedaliah was the new governor in Judah. He seemed to be a good man. His father once helped to keep Jeremiah from being put to death.

The people who were left in the land heard that Gedaliah was governor. They gathered to him. Gedaliah told them not to be afraid to serve the Chaldeans. He told them to live in the land, and things would go well for them.

By this time there were Jews scattered in many parts of the world. They heard that a few Jews were left in Jerusalem. When they heard that Gedaliah was governor, they returned to Jerusalem. They gathered in wine and many summer fruits, according to the command of Gedaliah.

One of the men who had come back with the other Jews was Ishmael. Some of the captains came to Gedaliah and warned him about Ishmael. They told him that Ishmael had been sent to kill him. But Gedaliah did not believe what they said.

Johanan spoke secretly to Gedaliah. He said, "Please let me go, and I will kill Ishmael. No man shall know about it. Why should he kill you? And why should he cause all the Jews which have been gathered to you to become scattered and die?"

Gedaliah answered, "You shall not do this thing. You are speaking falsely about Ishmael."

Some time later, Ishmael and ten other men came to the place where Gedaliah was. They ate bread with him. Then Ishmael and the ten men who were with him arose. They killed Gedaliah with the sword. They also killed the Jews and the men of war who were there with him.

Two days passed. Still no one else knew what had happened. Eighty men from a distance came with offerings to the house of the Lord. Ishmael went out to meet them. He was weeping as he went. When he met them, he said, "Come to Gedaliah." When they came into the city, Ishmael killed them. He threw them into a pit. There were ten men among them who said to Ishmael, "Do not kill us. We have brought treasures of wheat, barley, oil, and honey in the field." So Ishmael did not kill these men.

Ishmael took captive all the people who were left there and started out for another country.

Johanan and the captains who were with him heard about the evil that Ishmael had done. They went to fight with him. They found him by the great waters which are in Gibeon. When all the people who were with Ishmael saw Johanan and the captains who were with him, they were glad.

All the people whom Ishmael had carried away captive turned around and went with Johanan. But Ishmael escaped from Johanan with eight men.

The People Go to Egypt

Jeremiah 41:16–43:7

Johanan and the people with him got ready to go down into Egypt. They were afraid to stay in Judah because Ishmael had killed the governor whom the king of Babylon had set over them.

First they went to the prophet Jeremiah to see what advice he would give them. They said to him, "Please do what we ask of you. Pray to the Lord your God for us. Pray for all who are left. Ask the Lord your God to show us what we should do."

Jeremiah said to them, "I have heard you. I will pray to the Lord your God as you have said. Whatever the Lord says, I will tell you. I will keep nothing back from you."

They said to Jeremiah, "The Lord watch between us if we do not do all that the Lord says. Whether it is good or evil, we will obey the voice of the Lord our God so that it may be well with us."

After ten days the Lord showed Jeremiah

what to answer these men. He called for Johanan and all the people. He said to them, "This is what the Lord God of Israel says: 'If you will stay in this land, then I will build you up. I will not pull you down. I will plant you and not pluck you up. I have turned from the evil that I have done to you. Do not be afraid of the king of Babylon. I am with you to save you. I will deliver you from his hand. I will show mercies to you and cause you to return to your own land.'"

Jeremiah warned the people, "Do not say, 'We will not live in this land. We will not obey the voice of the Lord our God. No, but we will go into the land of Egypt. There we shall see no war nor hear the sound of the trumpet. We will not get hungry for bread. There we will live.'

"The Lord says if you determine to go to Egypt to live, then the sword which you fear shall overtake you. The famine which you feared shall follow close after you. And there in Egypt ye shall die."

Then Jeremiah reminded the people that they had promised to do whatever the Lord said. Jeremiah told them that they were only pretending when they said they would obey. He told them that he knew they would not obey the

Lord. Because of this, they could be sure that all of them would die in the place where they went to live for a while.

Jeremiah told the people all the words which the Lord had told him. When he was through speaking to the people, the proud men said to Jeremiah, "You speak falsely. The Lord our God has not sent you to tell us not to go to Egypt. Baruch sets you against us. He wants to let the Chaldeans come and take us captive and put us to death."

Johanan and the captains gathered all who remained in Judah. They went down to the land of Egypt. They took Jeremiah and Baruch along.

Pronunciation Symbols
Used in the Glossary

/ā/   as in *pay*   /a/   as in *hat*

/ē/   as in *see*   /e/   as in *yes*

/ī/   as in *by*   /i/   as in *sit*

/ō/   as in *go*   /o/   as in *top*

/ū/   as in *cube*   /u/   as in *bug*

/o͞o/   as in *food*   /oo/   as in *foot*

/ou/   as in *out*   /sh/   as in *she*

/oi/   as in *boy*   /ch/   as in *chop*

/ô/   as in *saw*   /wh/   as in *when*

/ä/   as in *park*   /th/   as in *thin*

/ė/   as in *her*   /<u>th</u>/   as in *that*

/ə/   the indefinite vowel   /ng/   as in *sing*

     sound heard in an   /zh/   as in *measure*

     unaccented syllable,

     representing any of

     the five vowels, as in

     alone, listen, flexible,

     consider, suppose

Glossary

Abednego (ə·bed′nē·gō) *noun:* The Chaldean name given to Azariah in Babylon

Abiathar (ə·bī′ə·thär) *noun:* A high priest of the family of Eli

Abijah (ə·bī′jä) *noun:* **1.** King Jeroboam's son who died young **2.** King Rehoboam's son who became the second king of Judah

Abishai (ab′i·shī) *noun:* Joab's brother

Absalom (ab′sə·lom) *noun:* A beautiful son of David

abundance (ə·bun′dəns) *noun:* A great plenty

accused (ə·kūzd′) *verb:* Blamed

Adonijah (ad·ō·nī′jä) *noun:* The fourth son of David

affairs (ə·fārz′) *noun:* Any business or thing that is done or is to be done

Ahab (ā′hab) *noun:* A wicked king of Israel

Ahaz (ā′haz) *noun:* The son of King Jotham and a very wicked king of Judah

Ahaziah (ā·hə·zī′ä) *noun:* **1.** Ahab's son who was king of Israel **2.** The sixth king of Judah

Ahijah (ə·hī′jä) *noun:* A prophet of Shiloh

Ahithophel (ə·hith′ō·fel) *noun:* A man to whom David went for advice

351

alas (ə·las′)   *interjection:* An exclamation of sorrow, grief, pity, or regret

algum (al′gum)   *noun:* A kind of tree

Amalekite (am′ə·lek·īt)   *noun:* A tribe of people from the wilderness of Sinai

Amasa (am′ə·sä)   *noun:* A nephew of David

Amaziah (am·ə·zī′ä)   *noun:* The ninth king of Judah and son of Joash

Ammon (am′on)   *noun:* A heathen nation

Amnon (am′non)   *noun:* The oldest son of David

Amon (am′on)   *noun:* A wicked king of Judah who was the son of Manasseh

apes (āps)   *noun:* Animals similar to monkeys

Aphek (ā′fek)   *noun:* A walled city in Syria

appointed (ə·point′ed)   *verb:* Chosen and given a certain task to do

appreciated (ə·prē′shē·āt·ed)   *verb:* Felt thankfulness

Arabians (ə·rā′bē·ənz)   *noun:* People of Arabia, a country south and east of Israel and Judah

Asa (ā′sä)   *noun:* The king of Judah after his father Abijah

Asahel (ās′ə·hel)   *noun:* A nephew of David and brother of Joab

Athaliah (ath·ə·lī′ä)   *noun:* A daughter of Ahab and Jezebel, and wicked wife of Jehoram, king of Judah

Baal (bā′əl) *noun:* An idol or god of the people of Canaan which the children of Israel also worshiped at times

Baalim (bā′ləm) *noun:* Another name for the heathen god Baal, meaning more than one

Baasha (bā′ə•shə) *noun:* The third king of Israel, who lived during the time that Asa was king of Judah

Babylon (bab′ə•lən) *noun:* The capital city of Assyria

bandaged (ban′dājd) *verb:* Covered or dressed with soft cloth or something to heal

Baruch (bā′rook) *noun:* A friend and fellow prisoner of Jeremiah

Barzillai (bär•zil′ā•ī) *noun:* An aged man who showed kindness to David

basins (bā′sinz) *noun:* wide, shallow dishes for holding liquid

Bath-sheba (bath•shē′bə) *noun:* The wife of Uriah who later became David's wife

Beer-sheba (bēr•shē′bə) *noun:* A city in southern Palestine

Belial (bē′li•əl) *noun:* Worthlessness; wickedness

Belshazzar (bel•shaz′ər) *noun:* A grandson of Nebuchadnezzar who became king of Babylon

Belteshazzar (bel′tə•shaz′ər) *noun:* The Chaldean name given to Daniel in Babylon

Benaiah (bē•nā′yä) *noun:* The son of a priest

Ben-hadad (ben•hā′dad) *noun:* A king of Syria

bored (bōrd) *verb:* Made a hole with a tool that turns as a drill

boughs (bouz) *noun:* Large branches of a tree

bracelet (brās′let) *noun:* Band worn around the wrist or arm

bullock (bool′ok) *noun:* An ox or a steer

capital (kap′i•tǝl) *noun:* **1.** The city where the people who rule the land live and work **2.** A capital letter

captive (kap′tiv) *noun:* A prisoner (He may not always be in prison, but may be taken away from his own home and forced to live somewhere else.)

captured (kap′chǝrd) *verb:* Taken as a prisoner by force

casket (kas′ket) *noun:* Coffin; a box in which a dead body is buried

castles (kas′ǝlz) *noun:* **1.** Palaces or fine homes **2.** Towers or buildings with thick walls for protection

cedar (sē′dǝr) *noun:* A cone-bearing tree whose wood is red and has a pleasant odor

ceiling (sē′ling) *noun:* The top of the inside of a room

celebration (sel•ǝ•brā′shǝn) *noun:* A service or feast in honor of someone or something

Chaldean (kal•dē′ǝn) **1.** *adjective:* Of the country of which Babylon was the capital **2.** *noun:* A person who lived in the land of Babylon

Cherith (ker′ith) *noun:* The brook where Elijah was fed by ravens

354

cherubims (cher′ū•bimz) *noun:* Heavenly beings; angels

Chimham (chim′ham) *noun:* A friend of David

collection (kə•lek′shən) *noun:* Something that is gathered together

commotion (kə•mō′shən) *noun:* A disturbance

comparison (kəm•par′ə•sən) *noun:* Consideration of the likeness or difference between two or more things

compassion (kəm•pash′ən) *noun:* A loving feeling of pity

congregation (kong•grē•gā′shən) *noun:* A group of people gathered together for worship or instruction

considered (kən•sid′ərd) *verb:* Thought about

container (kən•tān′ər) *noun:* A box, can, dish, or other vessel used to hold something

continue (kən•tin′ū) *verb:* Keep on

counselors (koun′səl•ərz) *noun:* People who give advice

covetous (kuv′ə•tus) *adjective:* Wanting something that belongs to another

Cushi (kū′shi) *noun:* A messenger who carried news to David

cushion (koosh′ən) *noun:* A soft pillow or pad

Damascus (də•mas′kus) *noun:* The capital city of Syria about 130 miles northeast of Jerusalem

debt (det) *noun:* Something that is owed to another

dedicated (ded′i•kāt•əd) *verb:* Set apart for a special purpose

defend (dē•fend′) *verb:* To guard in order to keep from harm

defile (dē•fīl′) *verb:* To make filthy or dirty

degrees (dē•grēz′) *noun:* Divisions of measurement on a scale

deliver (dē•liv′ər) *verb:* To set free from evil or danger

deliverance (dē•liv′ər•əns) *noun:* Salvation

denied (dē•nīd′) *verb:* Said that something was not true

descendant (dē•send′ənt) *noun:* A child or grandchild or someone from a following generation in a family

diet (dī′et) *noun:* The food which one eats

disguise (dis•gīz′) *verb:* To change the looks of someone or something so it is not recognized

Dothan (dō′thən) *noun:* A town in the land of Canaan

dungeon (dun′jən) *noun:* A dark underground prison

Ebed-melech (ē•bed′ mə•lek) *noun:* an Ethiopian man who helped Jeremiah

Ecclesiastes (ē•klē•zē•as′tēz) *noun:* A book of the Bible written by Solomon (This title means "the preacher.")

Elah (ē′lä) *noun:* The son of Baasha who ruled Israel after his father for parts of two years

Elijah (ē•lī′jä) *noun:* A prophet of God who performed many miracles in Israel

356

Elisha (ē•lī′shä)   *noun:* A prophet of God who took Elijah's place when Elijah went to heaven

encourage (en•kėr′āj)   *verb:* To give hope and courage

engines (en′jənz)   *noun:* Devices used to shoot arrows and stones

entrance (en′trəns)   *noun:* A place to go in

escaped (e•skāpt)   *verb:* Got free; got away from danger

especially (es•pesh′əl•ē)   *adverb:* More than others; particularly

Ethiopian (ē•thē•ō′pē•ən)   *noun:* Someone from the country of Ethiopia; a Negro

ewe (ū)   *noun:* A female sheep

experience (ik•spēr′ē•əns)   **1.** *noun:* Something that happens to a person   **2.** *verb:* To go through a happening

famous (fā′mus)   *adjective:* Very well known; much talked about

ferry (fer′ē)   *noun:* A boat used to carry people and goods across a body of water

fiery (fīr′ē)   *adjective:* Blazing with fire

filthiness (filth′ē•nəs)   *noun:* Extreme dirtiness

fleeing (flē′ing)   *verb:* Running away

forsook (fôr•sook′)   *verb:* Turned away from

fulfilled (ful•fild′)   *verb:* Brought to pass; accomplished

furiously (fūr′ē·us·lē) *adverb:* Wildly or with great speed

furnace (fėr′nəs) *noun:* A closed-in place to keep a fire

Gedaliah (ged·ə·lī′ä) *noun:* A governor of Judah and a friend of Jeremiah

Gehazi (ge·hā′zī) *noun:* A servant of Elisha

generations (jen·ə·rā′shənz) *noun:* The steps in a family (Your grandparents are one generation, your parents the next generation, and you are the next generation)

Gihon (gī′hon) *noun:* A pool near Jerusalem

Gilboa (gil·bō′ä) *noun:* The mountain where Saul and Jonathan were slain

gourds (gôrdz) *noun:* **1.** The hard-shelled fruit of some plants **2.** Plants such as pumpkin, squash, and cucumber vines

gracious (grā′shus) *adjective:* Pleasant, kind, and courteous

guests (gests) *noun:* Visitors; people whom you keep or entertain

guilt (gilt) *noun:* Fact of having done wrong

gushed (gusht) *verb:* Poured forth suddenly

Hananiah (han·ə·nī′ä) *noun:* **1.** The Hebrew name for Shadrach, one of Daniel's three companions **2.** A false prophet who lived in the time of Jeremiah

handsome (han′som) *adjective:* Good-looking

Hanun (hā′nun) *noun:* The son of Nahash who became king of the Ammonites after his father

hasty (hāst′ē) *adjective:* In a hurry

Hazael (hā′zā•el) *noun:* A king of Syria

hearth (härth) *noun:* The floor of a fireplace; fireside

heathen (hē′thən) *noun:* One who does not believe in God or the Bible

Hebron (hē′bron) *noun:* A town in the mountains of Judah, south of Jerusalem

herald (her′əld) *noun:* Someone who carries a message or makes an announcement

Hezekiah (hez•ə•kī′ä) *noun:* A good king of Judah who was the son of wicked Ahaz

Hilkiah (hil•kī′ä) *noun:* A priest who was the father of the prophet Jeremiah

Hiram (hī′rəm) *noun:* King of Tyre who loved David

history (hist′ə•rē) *noun:* Story of what has happened in the past

hold (hōld) **1.** *noun:* A castle, fort, or strong place **2.** *verb:* To keep in one's hands; keep in place

homeland (hōm′land) *noun:* The country that is one's home

Horeb (hôr′eb) *noun:* The mountain of God; Mount Sinai

Hoshea (hō•shē′ə) *noun:* The last king of Israel

household (hous'hōld) *noun:* All the family and servants living at a house; sometimes including their business affairs also

humbled (hum'bəld) *verb:* Brought low in feelings; put away pride

Hushai (hōō'shā·ī) *noun:* A friend of David

incense (in'sens) *noun:* A perfume that gives off a sweet smell when it is burned

industrious (in·dus'trē·us) *adjective:* Hardworking; the opposite of lazy

inheritance (in·her'i·təns) *noun:* Something received from one's parents or someone who died

innocent (in'ə·sənt) *adjective:* Not guilty

Isaiah (ī·zā'ä) *noun:* A prophet of God who lived in the time of several kings of Israel and Judah

Ish-bosheth (ish'bō·sheth) *noun:* The youngest of Saul's four sons, who became king after him

Ittai (it'ā·ī) *noun:* A stranger who wanted to be loyal to David

ivory (ī'vôr·ē) *noun:* The hard, white part of animal tusks (Elephants have ivory tusks.)

Jabesh (jā'besh) *noun:* A short name for Jabesh-gilead

Jabesh-gilead (jā'besh·gil'ē·əd) *noun:* A town east of the Jordan River

Jehoahaz (jē•hō′ə•haz) *noun:* **1.** The king of Israel after Jehu **2.** The king of Judah after Josiah

Jehoash (jē•hō′ash) *noun:* The twelfth king of Israel and son of Jehoahaz

Jehoiachin (jē•hoi′ə•kin) *noun:* The son of Jehoiakim who was king only a short time

Jehoiada (jē•hoi′ə•dä) *noun:* A good high priest who was a great help to King Joash

Jehoiakim (jē•hoi′ə•kim) *noun:* The son of Josiah and the eighteenth king of Judah

Jehoram (jē•hō′rəm) *noun:* **1.** One of the kings of Judah **2.** One of the kings of Israel, also called Joram

Jehoshaphat (jē•hosh′ə•fat) *noun:* A good king of Judah

Jehu (jē′hū) *noun:* A king of Israel

Jeroboam (jer•ō•bō′əm) *noun:* The first king of Israel after Israel and Judah were divided

Jezebel (jez′ə•bel) *noun:* The wicked wife of King Ahab

Jezreel (jez′rē•el) *noun:* The city where Ahab had his royal home

Joab (jō′ab) *noun:* David's nephew and the captain of his army

Joash (jō′ash) *noun:* A king of Judah who was a good king as long as the good priest Jehoiada lived

Johanan (jō•hā′nən) *noun:* A captain in Jerusalem when Gedaliah was governor

Joppa (jop′ə) *noun:* An old city by the Mediterranean Sea, about thirty miles northwest of Jerusalem

Joram (jō′rəm) *noun:* A short form of the name Jehoram

Josiah (jō•sī′ä) *noun:* A very good king of Judah

Jotham (jō′thəm) *noun:* The son of Uzziah and a good king of Judah

juniper (jōō′ni•pər) *noun:* An evergreen tree with small cones

Kidron (kid′ron) *noun:* the brook between Jerusalem and the Mount of Olives

Kishon (kī′shon) *noun:* A river that empties into the sea at the foot of Mount Carmel

lamentations (lam•en•tā′shənz) *noun:* Cries of sorrow

lattice (lat′is) *noun:* Crossed wooden or metal strips with open spaces between

Lebanon (leb′ə•non) *noun:* The highest and best known mountain range of Syria, north of Israel

magnificent (mag•nif′ə•sənt) *adjective:* Splendid and grand

magnified (mag′ni•f īd) *verb:* **1.** Increased the apparent size **2.** Praised; exalted

Manasseh (ma•nas′ä) *noun:* The son of Hezekiah and a very wicked king of Judah who later humbled himself

mantle (man′təl) *noun:* A cape or cloak without sleeves

masons (māˈsənz) *noun:* Builders with stone or brick

Melzar (melˈzär) *noun:* A master over Daniel and his three friends

Mephibosheth (me·fibˈō·sheth) *noun:* The lame son of Jonathan

Meshach (mēˈshack) *noun:* The Chaldean name of Mishael, one of Daniel's three companions

Michaiah (mī·kāˈyä) *noun:* A good prophet of the Lord

Mishael (mishˈē·əl) *noun:* The Hebrew name for Meshach

mistress (misˈtres) *noun:* A woman who has maids working for her

molten (mōltˈən) *adjective:* Melted, and shaped by pouring into a mold

Moriah (mō·rīˈä) *noun:* One of the hills of Jerusalem on which Solomon built the temple

Mount Olivet (mount olˈi·vet) *noun:* A mountain on the east of Jerusalem

Mount Seir (mount sēˈər) *noun:* The mountains south of the Dead Sea

mulberry (mulˈber·ē) *noun:* A small berrylike fruit that grows on a tree

mules (mūlz) *noun:* Animals that are part horse and part donkey

Naaman (nāˈə·mən) *noun:* A captain of the Syrian army who was a leper

Naboth (nā'both)   *noun:* An Israelite who owned a vineyard near Ahab's palace

Nadab (nā'dab)   *noun:* A king of Israel

Nathan (nā'thən)   *noun:* A prophet of the Lord in the time of David

naughty (nô'tē)   *adjective:* Disobedient, bad

Nebat (nē'bat)   *noun:* A man of Israel who was the father of Jeroboam

Nebuchadnezzar (neb•ū•kad•nez'ər)   *noun:* A great king of Babylon

Nebuzaradan (neb•ū•zär'ə•dən)   *noun:* A chief bodyguard of Nebuchadnezzar

neglect (nē•glekt')   *verb:* To leave undone; not care for

nephew (nef'ū)   *noun:* The son of one's brother, brother-in-law, sister, or sister-in-law

Obadiah (ō•bə•dī'ä)   *noun:* An officer of King Ahab who feared the Lord and helped hide the Lord's prophets

Obed-edom (ō•bed•ē'dom)   *noun:* A man who kept the ark of God for a time

Omri (om'ri)   *noun:* The commander of Elah's armies who took the kingdom of Israel from Zimri when Elah was killed

opinion (ō•pin'yən)   *noun:* An idea thought to be right

Ornan (or'nən)   *noun:* A man who owned a threshing floor at Jerusalem

pardon (pär′don)   *verb:* To forgive

Pashur (pash′ər)   *noun:* Chief governor of the house of the Lord and an enemy of Jeremiah

peaceably (pē′sə•blē)   *adverb:* With peace; pleasantly

peacocks (pē′koks)   *noun:* Large birds with beautiful green, blue, and gold feathers

permission (pər•mish′ən)   *noun:* Consent; word that something is allowed

persuaded (pər•swād′əd)   *verb:* Urged and won over to do or believe

pestilence (pes′tə•ləns)   *noun:* Any disease that causes many deaths

plague (plāg)   *noun:* A dangerous disease that spreads rapidly and kills many

pleaded (plēd′əd)   *verb:* Begged earnestly

pluck (pluck)   *verb:* To pull out or off; pick

possession (pō•zesh′ən)   *noun:* **1.** Ownership **2.** Something that is owned

privileges (priv′ə•lij•əz)   *noun:* Special favors or benefits

prophecy (prof′ə•sē)   *noun:* A prophet's message; prediction of what will happen in the future

prophesy (prof′ə•sī)   *verb:* To tell what will happen in the future

protested (prō•test′əd)   *verb:* Spoke against; showed disagreement

Proverbs (prov′ərbz)   *noun:* A book of the Bible; wise sayings written mostly by Solomon

provoke (prō·vōk′)   *verb:* To stir up anger

Rabshakeh (rab·shā′kə)   *noun:* A man sent by the king of Assyria to frighten the people of Judah

Ramoth-gilead (rā′moth·gil′ē·ad)   *noun:* One of the chief cities east of the Jordan in the land of Gad

rebelled (rē·beld′)   *verb:* Fought or worked against

Rechabites (rek′ə·bīts)   *noun:* People of the family of Rechab

redemptive (rē·demp′tiv)   *adjective:* Saving from sin

Rehoboam (rē·hō·bō′əm)   *noun:* Solomon's son who reigned after him

reigned (rānd)   *verb:* Ruled

request (rē·kwest′)   **1.** *verb:* To ask for something **2.** *noun:* The thing that is asked for

responsibility (rē·spon·sə·bil′ə·tē)   *noun:* The thing for which one is responsible

responsible (rē·spon′sə·bəl)   *adjective:* Expected to take reward or blame for what is done

restore (rē·stōr′)   *verb:* To bring or give back

revealed (rē·vēld)   *verb:* Shown or made known

revealer (rē·vēl′ər)   *noun:* Someone who shows what was not known

righteous (rī′chus)   *adjective:* right and just

roll (rōl) *noun:* The kind of book used in Bible times; a long piece of paper rolled up

rumor (rōo′mər) *noun:* Something that is talked about with no proof that it is true

sackcloth (sak′klôth) *noun:* Cloth made of dark goats' hair, worn to show mourning or distress

Samaria (sə•mā′rē•ə) *noun:* **1.** The Northern Kingdom, also called Israel **2.** The capital city of the kingdom of Samaria or Israel

sanctify (sank′tē•fī) *verb:* To make holy; make free from sin

sanctuary (sank′chōo•er·ē) *noun:* A church or holy place; the part of the temple where the ark was kept

scorched (skôrcht) *verb:* Made brown or black from heat

scorpions (skôr′pē•ənz) *noun:* **1.** Animals like small lobsters that have stings in their tails **2.** Whips that have sharp barbs in the lashes

scribe (skrīb) *noun:* A writer

separated (sep′ə•rāt•əd) *verb:* Divided; put apart

sepulcher (sep′əl•kər) *noun:* Tomb or grave; place of burial

servants (sėr′vənts) *noun:* People who work for others

Shadrach (shā′drak) *noun:* The Chaldean name for Hananiah, one of Daniel's three companions

sheath (shēth) *noun:* A case or covering for the blade of a sword or knife

Sheba (shē′bə) *noun:* **1.** A man who tried to take the kingdom from David **2.** A land far to the south of Israel

Shechem (shē′kem) *noun:* An important city in the hills of Samaria

sheepshearers (shēp′shēr•ərz) *noun:* Workers who cut the coat of wool off sheep

Shemaiah (shē•mā′yä) *noun:* A prophet who lived when Rehoboam was king

sheriffs (sher′ifs) *noun:* Officers appointed to keep order

shewbread (shō′bred) *noun:* Loaves put on the table in the tabernacle for the priests

Shimei (shim′ē•ī) *noun:* A man of the tribe of Benjamin

shred (shred) *verb:* To cut or tear into fine pieces

Shunammite (shoo′nə•mīt) *noun:* A person from the city of Shunem

Shunem (shoo′nəm) *noun:* A city near Jezreel

silo (sī′lō) *noun:* A tower used to store food for animals

singed (sinjd) *verb:* Burned a little at the edges or ends

skull (skul) *noun:* The bones of the head

smite (smīt) *verb:* To strike or hit; destroy

Solomon (sol′o•mon) *noun:* Son of David and Bath-sheba, known for his great wisdom

spied (spīd) *verb:* Caught sight of

spies (spīz) **1.** *noun:* More than one spy **2.** *verb:* Watches secretly

spy (spī) **1.** *noun:* A person who keeps secret watch on something **2.** *verb:* To keep secret watch

startling (stärt′ling) *adjective:* Causing sudden surprise or alarm

starve (stärv) *verb:* To die from lack of food

staves (stāvz) *noun:* Sticks; more than one staff

stocks (stoks) *noun:* A wooden frame with holes in which to put a prisoner's feet and sometimes his hands, used as a punishment

sundial (sun′dī•əl) *noun:* Something used to tell time by a shadow made by the sun

surrounded (sə•round′əd) *verb:* Gone all the way around

suspected (su•spekt′əd) *verb:* Thought something was true with no evidence to prove it

Syrians (sir′ē•ənz) *noun:* People who live in the country of Syria

talents (tal′əntz) *noun:* **1.** Weights of gold or silver worth a great deal **2.** Abilities that God has given

Tarshish (tär′shish) *noun:* A city along the Mediterranean Sea to which ships were often sent

Tekoa (tē•kō′ä) *noun:* A town six miles south of Bethlehem and the area around it

thrice (thrīs) *adverb:* Three times

thrust (thrust) *verb:* Push with force

tongs (tongz) *noun:* A scissorslike tool with two arms used for lifting or handling things

treason (trē′zən) *noun:* Unfaithfulness to one's country or ruler

treasurers (trezh′ər•ərz) *noun:* Officers appointed to take care of money

Tyre (tīr) *noun:* A city by the Mediterranean Sea in the land north of Israel

unsuitable (un•sōō′tə•bəl) *adjective:* Not proper

Uriah (ū•rī′ä) *noun:* Husband of Bath-sheba

Uzzah (uz′ä) *noun:* A man who helped bring the ark to Jerusalem

Uzziah (u•zī′ä) *noun:* The son of Amaziah and a good king of Judah

valiant (val′yent) *adjective:* Brave; strong and full of courage

valuable (val′ū•ə•bəl) *adjective:* Worth a great price; important

vessels (ves′əlz) *noun:* Containers such as jars, pots, and bowls

weapons (wep′ənz) *noun:* Tools used for fighting or to protect

witchcraft (wich′kraft) *noun:* Power or deeds of witches

withstand (with•stand') *verb:* Work or stand against

yield (yēld) *verb:* To give up or give in

Zadok (zā'dok) *noun:* A high priest in the time of David

Zarephath (zar'ē•fath) *noun:* A town along the seacoast between Tyre and Zidon

Zechariah (zek•ə•rī'ä) *noun:* **1.** A son of the priest Jehoiada who spoke out against idolatry **2.** A prophet who lived during the time of the last kings of Judah

Zedekiah (zed•ə•kī'ä) *noun:* A son of Josiah and the last king of Judah

Ziba (zī'bä) *noun:* A servant of Saul

Zidon (zī'don) *noun:* A wealthy city along the Mediterranean Sea, north of Tyre

Zimri (zim'rī) *noun:* The fifth king of Israel who reigned only seven days

Glossary Words Arranged by Lessons

Unit 1

1

Amalekite
bracelet
continue
escaped
Gilboa

2

Asahel
Hebron
homeland
inheritance
Ish-bosheth
Jabesh
Jabesh-gilead
Joab
peaceably
persuaded
reigned

3

accused
casket
guilt
sackcloth

4

cedar
Hiram
masons

5

deliverance
hold
mulberry
Obed-edom
staves
Uzzah

6

magnified
Nathan

7

Ammon
Hanun
Mephibosheth
spy
Ziba

8

Bath-sheba
Syrians
Uriah

9

ewe

10

gracious
Solomon

11

Absalom
Amnon
fleeing
mules
nephew
sheepshearers

12

Ahithophel
handsome
spies

30

Ahijah
alas

history
industrious

Jeroboam
Rehoboam

Unit 2

1

capital
Samaria
scorpions
Shechem
Shemaiah

2

humbled
incense
Nebat
righteous

3

Josiah
restore

5

Abijah
disguise
provoke

6

Asa
Baasha
captured

Nadab
shewbread
withstand

7

Ahab
Elah
heathen
Jehoshaphat
Jezebel
Omri
valuable
Zimri

8

Cherith
Elijah
Zarephath
Zidon

9

Obadiah

10

bullock
gushed

Kishon
opinion

11

Horeb
Jezreel
juniper

12

Damascus
Elisha
entrance
Hazael
Jehu
mantle

13

Amon
Ben-hadad
comparison

15

Naboth

Unit 3

thrice
Zechariah

7

engines
Isaiah
Jotham
redemptive
tongs
Uzziah
weapons

8

Ahaz
experience
filthiness
Hezekiah
neglect
sanctify

9

compassion
sanctuary
yield

10

Hoshea
Rabshakeh

11

rumor

12

Babylon
degrees
sundial

13

Baalim
Manasseh
witchcraft

14

fulfilled
prophecy

15

Abednego
Belteshazzar
Chaldean
defile
diet
Hananiah
Jehoahaz
Jehoiakim
Melzar
–Meshach
–Mishael
– Nebuchadnezzar
– Shadrach

16

hasty
suspected

17

revealed
revealer

18

counselors
fiery
furnace
herald
sheriffs
silo
treasurers

19

scorched
singed

21

Belshazzar

22

—Hilkiah
—Lamentations
Pashur
pleaded
stocks

23

forsook
Rechabites

24

Baruch
hearth